D1562098

Fish Mounts and Other Fish Trophies

Quebec brook trout, 7½ pounds, 27 inches long. Prepared in polyester resin by Ralph Morrill, Hamden, Connecticut. Photo by Sebastian Frenzi.

Fish Mounts and Other Fish Trophies

THE COMPLETE BOOK OF FISH TAXIDERMY

Second Edition

Edward C. Migdalski

Director, Outdoor Education
Yale University

JOHN WILEY & SONS, New York • Chichester • Brisbane • Toronto

Library of Congress Cataloging in Publication Data:

Migdalski, Edward C
  Fish mounts and other fish trophies.

  Published in 1960 under title: How to make fish mounts.
  Includes index.
  1. Fishes—Collection and preservation.   2. Taxidermy.
  I. Title.

QL618.6.M53   1981   579′.4   80-27829
ISBN 0-471-07990-1

Printed in the United States of America

10 9 8 7 6 5 4 3 2 1

To Ralph Morrill, pioneer developer of modern fish mounting methods, who was my instructor and advisor during my student days at Yale University's Peabody Museum of Natural History.

Preface

Every angler with more than just a passing interest in fishing can recall the occasion when he wished that his catch could be preserved. The prize was perhaps an unusually large example of a favorite game fish. Or it may have been an unusually beautiful specimen—well colored or well proportioned—which he pictured as an attractive piece of decor in office or home. Perhaps the trophy was of sentimental value in recalling the "trip of a lifetime." But in the end, the thought was sadly dismissed, perhaps with an audible sigh: "Too much trouble" or "Too much money" and usually, "How would you go about it, anyway?" This book will show the average angler how to go about it cheaply and easily—and have a lot of fun at the same time.

Many anglers must think twice before carting their fish to a taxidermist, for good craftsmanship is expensive. Even if he can afford it without undue strain on his pocketbook, the angler may be several days away from civilization and consequently will give up a fine trophy because he believes it is extremely difficult or greatly inconvenient to preserve the fish long enough to reach a taxidermist. Many young children would derive great value from making a collection of fishes, but they are discouraged from attempting it because of the common thought that the project is too complicated.

A single attitude is common to all—the prevailing thought that preserving and mounting fish is very difficult. It is not. That is why I have been induced to write this book. Any angler who has the ability to cast a line or wind a reel can preserve a prize catch—easily and at negligible cost. No outstanding scientific or artistic ability is required to produce a pleasing, decorative trophy by one of the many methods described on the following pages—information that is not easily obtainable elsewhere. The fisherman who is miles away from home will find that he can care for his prize fish by employing a method that requires little time and only a small space in his car, with no ice or refrigeration needed. Objections to monstrosities on the home walls can be changed dramatically by introducing a clean-cut plastic mount, without the ugly backboard present on most commercially mounted fish—a trophy with little weight that can be hung easily anywhere to fit in with the house plan or decorations. For those who want even simpler methods, I suggest an outline of the prize catch in wood or mounted on art board. Or the head, tail, or bill of the fish can be dried and preserved. And finally there is always the photograph, where a few practical hints can make all the difference between a stiff, unnatural picture and a pleasing record of a memorable event.

Children who have an interest in the outdoors are always attempting to form collections, and most of them try a hand at some sort of taxidermy. Parents whose children indicate such interest are fortunate, and they should encourage their offspring whenever possible. I have included methods of working with fish that can fit into the specific interests and capabilities of any age group of young enthusiasts. Twenty summers of experience have brought home to me the importance of nature study and museums in summer camps. Annually, at the approach of spring, I receive inquiries from high school and college students, and others having jobs at summer camps about establishing a program concerning fish. This has led me to include a complete section of instructions on collecting, preserving, and displaying a fish collection intelligently at summer camps and other holiday resorts—inland or along the seashore. An organized activity of this type can be of inestimable value to any summer camp.

As Ichthyologist and Chief Preparator of Fishes at Yale University's Peabody Museum and Bingham Oceanographic Laboratory for more than twenty years, I traveled around the world studying, photographing, collecting, and making molds of fishes, as well as producing the finished mounts for museum display. The expeditions, varied in time and objective, took place in India, Nepal, Africa, South America, New Zealand, Bermuda, Bahamas, Mexico, Newfoundland, Labrador, Nova Scotia, and many areas throughout the United States, including Alaska. Because of these expeditions, through trial and error, I have worked out different systems of preparing fishes in the field. Therefore, in Chapter 13, I have described these methods as well as the adventure and excitement involved in collecting some of the more exotic types; it should interest anyone seeking an insight into museum technology.

EDWARD C. MIGDALSKI

New Haven, Connecticut
February 1981

Contents

CHAPTER ONE

Field Care of Fishes

P lanning for an impressive trophy starts the moment the fish is landed. A few simple precautions at this stage can make all the difference between a first-class mount and a mess. None of these steps is difficult or complicated, but I have found from long experience that the results repay a little extra effort.

COLOR PHOTOS AND NOTES. A clear photographic color transparency is an invaluable reference item in the production of any type of fish mount. A fish loses its true color immediately after death, so it should be photographed while still alive or as soon as it comes out of the water. If the fish is not thoroughly exhausted and won't pose quietly, hit it smartly on the head. Often a rap of this kind will bring out a burst of vivid color that the fish would not display otherwise—but be ready with your camera because this is a momentary reaction. I have found that a 35mm camera is best for photographic work of this type; it does not require much room in a pocket or tackle box. Take a shot of the entire fish; fill the camera finder with it. Then, as close as possible, take individual shots of the head, body, fins, and tail. Turn the fish on its belly and photograph its topside, then reverse for a belly shot. Take at least two different exposures of every shot to ensure color perfection in the film.

Place the fish on the dock, bottom of the boat, or ground. Look through the finder and note that, unless it's a very cloudy day, light is reflected from the surface of the fish to the camera. This reflection must be eliminated or most of the true color will be lost. Twist and turn the camera slightly; move a foot or so in different directions. An angle to photograph the fish without reflections, or at least with a minimum of reflection, can always be found. This procedure is not difficult, and with a bit of practice results should be good. Check your local camera shop for polarizing camera lens filters that eliminate glare and reflection. Such filters are inexpensive and should be part of your camera equipment. If a camera is not available when the fish is

1

caught, a later shot will be of some value even though the vividness of color is gone. In this case, supplement the camera work with written notes as soon as you can obtain pencil and paper.

It is possible to get by with only a field sketch and color notes if you do not have a camera. I prefer to photograph the fish and supplement the pictures with copious notes on a sketch pad containing an outline of the fish. If you know what species are to be collected, sketch a rough outline of the fishes at home, using a reference book. An outline sketch of the fish facilitates the recording of color without confusion and saves time in the field. The outline need not be absolutely accurate, but the eye, lips, and all fins must be there. Jot the notes on the body of the fish sketch where the colors occur, or else put them around the drawing with lines drawn to the particular parts of the fish described.

PROTECTING THE SPECIMEN.   Protecting the specimen in the field saves much extra work later, whether the fish is intended for a skin mount or a cast. Whenever I collect fish for mounting, I take along a couple of burlap sacks. As soon as the desirable specimen is caught, the sack is soaked in water and wrapped around the fish. Two things are thus accomplished. First, the fish is kept cool and moist so drying or shriveling of the skin and fins is prevented. Second, the fins are protected from damage and no scales are lost. Above all, the intended mount should not be placed on a stringer. The body of the fish will rub against the stringer, another fish, or the side of the boat, causing irreparable damage to the skin or scales. Further, the lips will tear, and repair work will be necessary when it could have been avoided. If a sack is not handy, wet grass, leaves, or weeds can be used to cover the fish on all sides. A spot in the shade, protected from the sun, should be selected for temporary storage of the fish.

Even if nothing more than a silhouette trophy is desired, the fish should be protected in the same manner. A specimen dried by exposure to the sun or air shrinks and loses some of its natural features.

PREVENTING SPOILAGE.   Obviously, the angler's first concern after a day's fishing should be the prevention of spoilage to the intended mount. This can be accomplished by freezing or the use of Formalin. If both these methods prove unsatisfactory, the angler should skin the fish in the field and salt its skin thoroughly.

Freezing.   If time allows, the best method is to freeze the fish and keep it frozen until time for skinning or molding in plaster. Wrap the specimen in wet material before placing it in the freezer. The first layer should be a smooth-textured cloth dripping with water. Rough materials press irregularities into the fish's body that freeze and are difficult to remove when the

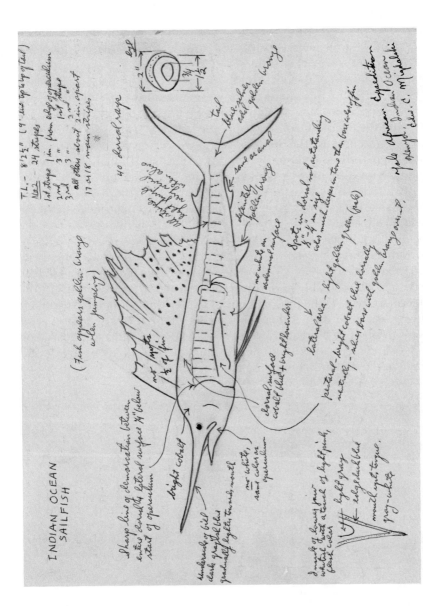

Figure 1. Recording the color of a specimen by camera is a necessity whenever possible, but field notes like those in this sketch are highly important as a safety factor, especially if the weather is bad, film exposure is not true, or film and camera are not at hand. Furthermore, the observable intensity of true coloration while the fish is alive before being boated can be noted on the sketch.

fish thaws out. Do *not* bind the cloth with twine or cord because this also marks the body. Allow the cloth to extend an inch or two beyond the tail; so the end of the tail is protected from bending when you fold back the excess cloth. Now place the wrapped fish on a wet potato sack and fold the sack around it. This heavy, wet sack will supply additional moisture and protection for the fish when it freezes into a solid package. Again be careful not to fold the end of the tail. Finally, encase the whole package in heavy wax paper used by meat markets for wrapping purposes. Bind the paper with pieces of tape, such as Scotch tape, so the package will not unwrap.

During the procedure of wrapping the fish, its "show side" should be kept in mind because the opposite side must be down when placing the specimen in the freezer. Usually the "down side" will flatten a bit, and this will make for difficulties in molding. Write "This side up" on the paper wrapper. If possible, have the fish placed on a flat surface in the freezer. All of these small details pay great dividends when it comes time to mold the fish. Of course, if the fish is to be skinned, such meticulous care of the specimen is not necessary.

Arrangements for freezing specimens can usually be made with some local food store, ice-cream plant, or person who has a freezer. Surprisingly, I have always been able to do this even in tiny towns located in remote wilderness areas. If the trophy requires two or three days in transit after being frozen, or if the weather is unusually warm, it is wise to stop at an ice-cream plant or dairy where a few slabs of dry ice and a cardboard box can be purchased. You should not hesitate to do so. I have always found people in these plants courteous and cooperative.

Figure 2. Note how the fins have been spread to show markings as a reference when painting the mount.

Figure 3. Alaskan chum salmon, ready to be wrapped in wet burlap as a protection against fin and scale damage, en route to base camp on the Yukon River.

During a trip from San Antonio, Texas, my wife Bo and I drove to Connecticut with two G.I. trunks of fish in our station wagon. My pal Larry Sheerin and I had flown back from a fishing trip in Mexico with snook and channel bass; then the three of us caught largemouth bass in Texas. We froze the fish, put them in the trunks, and placed several cakes of dry ice in each trunk. At regular intervals Bo and I stopped to replenish our supply of dry ice. Our leisurely return home required several days, but we had no trouble obtaining the ice for our fish. As a matter of fact, we found it fun.

Another time, George Albrecht and I were returning from a successful trip to the Miramachi River in Canada, and with us were fine specimens of a salmon and a grilse that we intended to mount. The fish were originally frozen in the freezer of a small general store in New Brunswick. We stopped at a motel for the night and talked to the manager about our fish. The manager and his wife not only accommodated our fish in their freezer overnight, but also invited us to dinner. We discovered that they were ardent fishermen themselves. Returning from distant areas while keeping fish frozen is a task which should not discourage any angler.

Formalin.   Another method of field preservation is the use of a powerful chemical called Formalin. It is a colorless liquid having a pungent odor and vapors that are intensely irritating to mucous membranes. Although

Formalin is invaluable to scientists in the field and laboratory, I recommend that children do not handle it without the direct supervision of an adult. Adult anglers who treat this chemical with respect and a bit of caution will find it advantageous for fish collection and preservation.

Before attempting this method I advise the angler to read about the use of Formalin in Chapter 15. When packing Formalin for shipment into the field, the glass jars should be well protected against breakage with excelsior, newspapers, or other material. I have packed Formalin for shipment to such distant places as India and Africa and not a drop was spilled in transit despite the rough handling freight aboard a ship receives.

The correct mixture for field preservation of fishes is a 10 per cent solution made from nine parts water to one part Formalin. A receptacle large enough to accommodate the specimen is required. A baby's bathtub or a washtub is ideal, though a piece of plastic cloth or rubberized material supported on the sides with earth and stones can be formed into a suitable container. Another method is to dig a shallow rectangular pit in the ground and place the waterproof material within it; it is ready to receive the Formalin and the fish.

Before the fish is placed in the Formalin, the dorsal and anal fins should be held in lifelike positions by pins inserted at their bases. If the intended mount is to have an open mouth, it should now be pried open, and a piece of wire or a twig placed in position so the jaws will have the desired opening. Once a fish has remained in Formalin for just a few hours, it is impossible to change the position of any part of the fish without damage. Within a day or two the fish is rigid and feels like hard rubber. Once preserved in position, it can be stored in Formalin in any convenient receptacle until the time to transport it home.

A freshly caught fish should have good belly contours. If the belly is sunken in a small fish, use a hypodermic syringe to inject full-strength (not diluted with water) Formalin into the fish's body cavity until the former roundness of the belly is restored. If a syringe is not available, slit the abdomen along the side of the fish opposite the show side, and fill the abdominal cavity with wet paper, cloth, moss, or any other appropriate material. The slit side of the fish should be placed down in the Formalin.

In the next day or so the specimen should be checked and two narrow strips of skin and flesh should be removed (lengthwise) from the side of the fish opposite the show side. This facilitates penetration of the Formalin into all parts of the fish before bacterial action takes place. A big trout or bass placed in a 10 per cent solution of Formalin is thoroughly preserved in a few days. The specimen, however, may remain safely immersed all summer or longer.

If it is inconvenient to bring the preserved fish home in a receptacle large enough to accommodate it in Formalin, the specimen can be transported

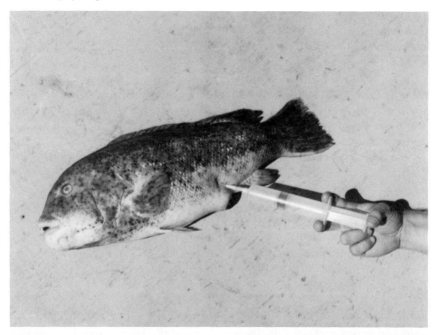

Figure 4. If necessary, inject Formalin or water into the body cavity to fill out its full contour before molding. In warm weather, if the fish is to be left overnight, inject a 10 percent solution of Formalin into the body cavity until the belly resumes its original shape.

wrapped in wet cloths or wet layers of paper. Wet moss can also be used. Any wooden box will hold the fish providing a top is securely on. A few layers of wax paper should be placed within the box so the wood does not absorb moisture. The fish will not spoil or go soft out of the Formalin, but it is of utmost importance to keep the specimen wet so shrinkage does not occur. Of course, the specimen must be put back in Formalin when you get home.

When you work with Formalin, water should be within easy reach in case hands come in contact with the chemical. Reaching for a fish in Formalin—if hands remain in the Formalin only long enough to remove the specimen—is not dangerous providing you wash your hands immediately with water. Using rubber gloves, however, will be safer. Formalin is extremely dangerous if splashed into eyes accidentally. If this occurs, run fresh water into the eyes immediately. Again, do not work with Formalin if you are not familiar with it; be sure to read about Formalin in Chapter 15.

Skinning in the Field.   The angler who finds it difficult to bring a trophy home in a frozen state or preserved in Formalin should skin the fish in the field before it gets soft, even if the intended mount is to be cast in plaster or in a synthetic material. In the event that a cast is desirable, the skin can be reconstructed in the home or laboratory so that a plaster mold of the fish can still be made (see Chapter 2).

For directions on field skinning, read the first section on skinning in Chapter 5, then return here. But before you start the actual skinning, make a careful outline drawing of the fish on a piece of wrapping paper. Photographs or measurements of the fish, or both, will also be of assistance in reconstructing the specimen. It is easy to stray from the form of the fish in reconstruction because a fish skin will stretch or move into different positions when the original, exact contours of measurements are not employed. If time is important, it is not necessary to clean and flesh the skin thoroughly in the field to preserve it for future mounting. If there is time and it does not interfere with fishing schedules, by all means do a finished job. But the finer points of removing every bit of flesh from the skin—around the bases of the fins, tail, head bones, and cheeks—are time consuming and not necessary if the angler is rushed. This part of the job is done much better later at home and at leisure.

Salting the Skin.   Thorough salting of the skin is important. Turn the skin inside out and use salt liberally around the base of the fins and tail. Rub salt well into all parts of the head, and then fill the head with another handful. Next, pile about an inch of salt over the entire fish. Turn back the sides to their original position and roll the skin into a ball, meanwhile adding still more salt. Then place another inch of salt on the bottom of a suitable container. A bait pail or a paint bucket is excellent. If a wooden box is used, place a couple of layers of wax paper around the inside. Place the rolled skin in the container and fill all the space around the fish with salt. Put the cover or lid of the container on solidly—results are best from airtight receptacles. The box or can should not be placed in the sun or next to a heated radiator.

I have used this method on several specimens during a lengthy collecting trip in Alaska. Upon returning to the laboratory, I placed the cans containing the fish skins in the deep freeze, just as they were. Two years later I removed the specimens; to my surprise, they were excellent to work with and the color retention of the skin amazed me. On another trip, I collected an important fish, a mahseer, high in the mountains of Nepal—a country between Tibet and India. This salted fish skin, in an airtight jar, traveled with me for weeks in the Himalayan Mountains, then through the heat of the Indian plains, and arrived many months later at Yale University in excellent condition. This method should be popular with anglers because the fish skin is safe to transport and takes up little room in a car. It can even be mailed home easily without worry.

CHAPTER TWO

Plaster Molds

O nce your fish has been brought away from the waterside with a minimum amount of damage, there are many different ways it can be transformed into a striking and decorative trophy. Perhaps the most realistic method is a cast produced from a mold of the entire fish.

MOLDS AND CASTS.   A mold and a cast are not the same thing, though the two are sometimes confused. A *mold* is the poured or flowed plaster that sets in a solid form around the object intended for reproduction. A mold may be constructed with rubber, specially mixed sands, glue, molding plaster, or other materials. In this volume we are concerned mainly with plaster molds. The *cast* is the object reproduced from the mold, a replica. In other words, a mold is the negative form from which the cast, a positive form or imitation of the original object, is reproduced.

In making fish molds, use only a Grade A or No. 1 molding plaster (plaster of Paris). Stay clear of the material used for wall plastering. (Plaster should not be confused with the cement mixed with sand and gravel to form concrete.) Molding plaster is used mostly by artists and museum workers for producing molds and casts that retain fine detail. The best grade of molding plaster, which resembles a pure white powder, costs about $10.00 for a 100-pound bag.

MIXING THE PLASTER.   Molding plaster must be mixed with care. Place the desired amount of water (the amount will vary with the size of the object to be molded) in a pan, bowl, or other receptacle. Do *not* place the plaster in the pan first. Sift the plaster into the water gradually with a scoop or trowel. Proceed to spread the plaster evenly over the entire surface of the water until the plaster no longer disappears—a light powdery layer should be obvious on the surface.

Now roll up your sleeve and run your hand slowly through the mixture until all the plaster that remained on the surface is blended in. While mixing, do not work your hand in and out of the plaster, nor stir vigorously or needlessly; an excessive formation of bubbles may arise. Squeeze all lumps that form until the entire mixture is smooth and fluid. Wipe away all bubbles that gather on the surface. The plaster is now ready for use.

MOLDING A FISH.   Read the entire section on molding before trying it.

A two-piece mold is usually made of any fish the size of a trout, salmon, bass, bluefish, striped bass, or perch. A one-piece mold is made when a medallion-type plaster cast is desired, when the skin is to be filled with plaster or other material, or when the fish is too large to turn over. Occasionally, an unusual job may require a mold composed of several pieces. For example, on the shores of Peru I molded a 3300-pound-plus giant manta measuring 18½ feet from wing tip to wing tip, which required a four-piece mold (see Chapter 13). Techniques employed in the field differ from those used at home or in the laboratory and will be discussed later in this section. However, let's review the basic steps first.

Remove Slime.   Unless the slime is removed from the surface of the specimen, the mold will be unsatisfactory because the plaster will not set solidly next to the skin and definition will be poor. This is not very important when the mold is intended for use as a form for mounting the skin, but it is extremely important when the mold will be cast. First, go over the entire fish with a brush and water. This will remove all excess dirt and slime. Then pour about half a pint of vinegar into a quart of water and go over the whole fish. Rinse the fish well with clean water. Next mix a handful of alum in a quart of water and again go over the fish. Pour the remaining alum water over the fish and let it remain on the specimen while preparing the next step. The alum has astringent qualities; that is, it tends to contract or bind organic tissues and helps to alleviate the problem of slime and the oozing of fluids in the skin. A saturated solution of salt and water rubbed on with a soft cloth works well on some types of fish. A solution of three parts water and one part baking soda applied with a sponge will also remove slime.

Another easier method is to wipe the fish dry with a cloth and then simply spray or brush a thin coat of lacquer over the specimen. Nearly all hardware stores carry small cans of lacquer that you spray by pressing a release button. Lacquer dries almost instantly and covers any slime on the fish. It is best to apply the lacquer to the show side when the fish is all set and positioned in plaster.

Show Side and Fins.   Choose the side to be shown in the mount (called the show side) and lay the fish down on the other side. Clip the pectoral and

Figure 5. Photograph your fish and take color notes before molding. This is a 12 pound trout taken in Connecticut.

Figure 6. The pectoral and ventral fins are cut off from the body.

11

Figure 7. Build a shelf of soil, sand, or asbestos around the fish to the middle of its body.

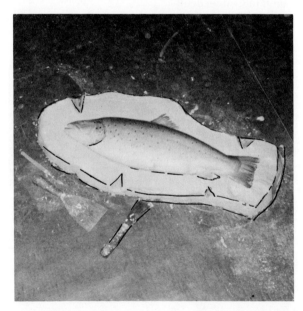

Figure 8. Cut two V-shaped keys or recesses along each side of the shelf. This can be done now or the keys can be cut into the plaster of the first half of the mold.

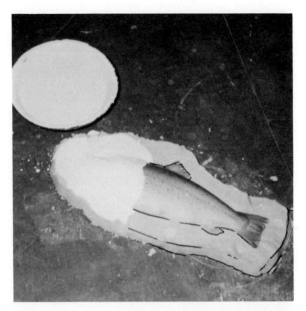

Figure 9. Flow the plaster over the fish. Start at the head or at the tail end.

Figure 10. Continue until the entire fish and the shelf are covered.

Figure 11. Molds of large fish should be reinforced with sisal. Cover the shelf first.

Figure 12. When the mold has set, turn it over and remove the material (asbestos, sand, or soil) from it.

Figure 13. Clean the shelf of the mold and apply the separator.

Figure 14. Proceed with the plaster, the same way on this side.

15

Figure 15. Also reinforce this side with sisal.

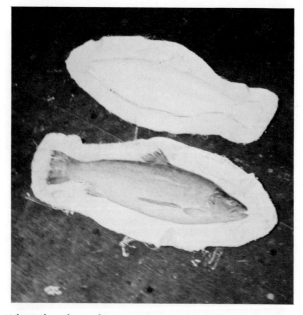

Figure 16. When the plaster has set, insert a chisel between the two halves and pry the mold apart.

16

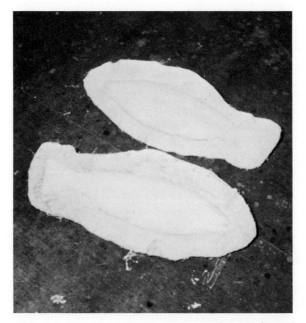

Figure 17.   Place the halves together and set aside to dry.

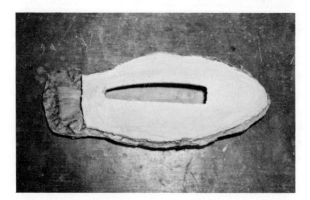

Figure 18.   The mold is ready for casting. Before cutting the rear side of the mold, as shown here, see Figs. 38 to 43.

17

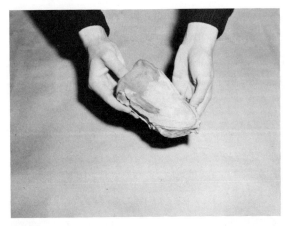

Figure 19. To make a separate mold of the open mouth, simply push a heavy mixture of plaster into it before making a mold of the body. Allow the plaster to set. Apply sterine separator over the mold of the mouth before placing plaster on the body.

   The mold of the mouth as removed from the fish. If the back end of the mold has holes or outstanding irregularities, correct them with modeling clay, as shown.

ventral fins close to their bases and set them aside in a glass of water so they don't dry out. A mold of these fins will be made later. Arrange the other fins in position. This is accomplished by inserting pins of pointed wire through the forepart of the fin and anchoring well into the body. Do not stretch the fins but position them so they look natural.

Belly Contour.   Next check the belly or abdominal contour. If it is sunken it should be filled either by an injection of water with a hypodermic syringe or by cutting a slit (opposite show side) and filling the abdominal cavity with pieces of cloth, newspaper, moss, or any other suitable material.

Shelf Around Fish.   Now place the fish on a table or the ground with its show side up and build a shelf of soil, sand, or asbestos—depending on where the work is taking place—completely around it to the midline (Fig. 7). On a fish the size of a 15-inch bass or trout, the shelf should extend out 3 or 4 inches. Cut two V-shaped keys or recesses (Fig. 8) along each side of this shelf. Keys will facilitate adjoining of the halves later. If the lacquer system is being used to cover slime, now is the time to apply it. The lacquer will be ready to receive the plaster before you finish mixing it.

Mold of Open Mouth.   With smaller fishes the mold of the mouth can be included with the first half of the mold by pushing plaster into the mouth.

In this case use care when removing the original fish from the mold so that the plaster, which forms the mold of the mouth, is not broken off. If it does break off, though, it can be glued back before casting the fish. After the cast is produced, the plaster in the mouth is dug out with appropriate small tools.

With a large fish, however, such as a 50-pound striped bass, it is better to make a separate mold of the mouth. Before applying plaster to the show side of the fish, push a heavy mixture of plaster well into the mouth. Allow it to set and apply sterine separator. After the mold of the whole fish has been completed, the mold of the mouth can then be separated from it.

Applying Plaster.   If the plaster is mixed in a large pan, use a smaller bowl to scoop up the plaster and convey it to the specimen. Flow the plaster over the fish evenly (Fig. 9). I prefer to apply the plaster by hand. Start at either the head or tail end and continue to the other end. Do not skip from one part of the fish to another. Be sure the plaster flows to the edges of the shelf so that no air pockets are formed. The entire fish should be covered quickly with a thin coat, often called the splash coat. Then the entire shelf should be covered. Start immediately again on one end and flow the remainder of the plaster over the entire fish. Enough plaster should be mixed in the first batch to cover the fish and the shelf to about a depth of ¾ inch. Do not disturb the mold until it sets, usually in about an hour. Notice that the mold heats perceptibly before setting; this warmth can be felt by placing the hand on the mold. Never disturb the mold before this action takes place—wait until the warmth is gone.

Now turn the fish and mold over to the other side. Remove the asbestos or sand (Fig. 14) and clean the hardened plaster that now forms a shelf around the specimen. Wipe the exposed side of the fish and give it a coat of lacquer (if using this method). Apply a separator to the shelf to prevent the flowing plaster from adhering to the set plaster. The separator may be Vaseline, sprayed lacquer or sterine applied with a brush. Mix another batch of plaster and repeat the process on this side of the fish.

Warning! Plaster sets fairly quickly. Do not diddle along while working. Clean the plaster mixing receptacles as soon as possible. First remove as much plaster as you can with your hand; then use a scrub brush and water to remove the thin layer remaining—but quickly!

Molding the Fins.   While the mold is setting, the pectoral fin and the two ventral fins, which were cut off earlier, can be attended to. Place them on a piece of glass, table top, or other smooth surface which has been greased with Vaseline or sterine separator. Flow the plaster over the fins. The three fins can be incorporated in one mold, but I prefer to mold each separately (Fig. 20). When the plaster has set, turn the molds over and cut two or three

Figure 20. The pectoral and ventral fins of a striped bass ready for molding. Brush sterine over the table top first so that the plaster will not adhere to it.

Figure 21. Cover each fin with plaster.

20

Figure 22. Molds of large fins should be reinforced with sisal.

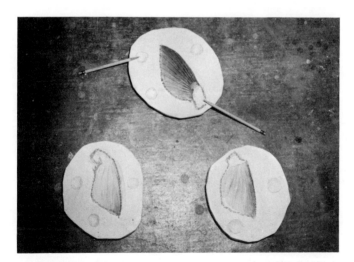

Figure 23. Left pencil points to conelike key which has been gouged out of the plaster. The right pencil points to the gouged-out area at the base of the fin; it will provide for an extension of the fin when it is cast. Do not remove the fins. Brush sterine over the mold and then apply plaster.

Figure 24. A two-piece mold is made.

Figure 25. The mold halves are separated and fins removed. Pencil points to the protruding area at the fin base, which has to be cut away level with the shelf of the mold.

22

keys into the plaster of each mold (Fig. 23). Apply the separator and flow the plaster over the half molds thus making each two-piece. When the plaster has set, insert a chisel between the halves and tap gently with a hammer; the halves will separate. Remove the fins and set aside the molds to dry.

Separating Mold Halves.   Now return to the fish mold, and check that it has set. Separate the halves by inserting a chisel here and there between the two parts. The halves should come apart easily unless an excessive amount of plaster was allowed to flow down over the first half of the mold during the plastering of the second part. If this is the case, the edges have to be scraped until the line of demarcation can be clearly seen between the halves. Insert the chisel again and the mold halves will part cleanly.

Remove the fish without damaging the mold detail. I usually start by carefully inserting a fingernail under a corner of the tail fin and then gradually pull the fish's body up and toward the head. Clear away any bits of plaster on and around the shelves of the mold that might prevent the halves from coming together snugly. Place the halves together and set the mold aside until dried and ready for casting. As a protection, I always tie wire around each end of the mold so that nosy people will not open it and run their fingernails over the inside. A mold set over a furnace will dry quickly. During summer when furnaces are shut off, the mold should be placed outdoors or in a room with open windows. The fish cannot be cast unless the mold has lost most of its moisture. A fish mold 2 or 3 feet long should be dry enough within two or three days if placed over a furnace or in a heated room.

MOLDING IN THE FIELD.   Molding techniques in the field and home or in the laboratory are basically the same, but through years of trial and error I have found modifications in the process which are advantageous in each situation. The best possible results in the eventual cast are obtained from a mold which is completed as soon as possible after the fish is caught, and that means the same day or the next morning. This method is a must for scientific museum workers, and more information on it is found in Chapter 13. However, an angler who is vacationing and lives in a tent, cabin, or cottage not too far from shore, may try a hand at field molding during a lull in the fishing day.

Select a spot in the shade, if possible, for the temporary laboratory. Fresh water is necessary. If a faucet is not handy, fill a barrel or some 5-gallon tins with water from a distant water tap or from the lake and transport the water to the spot where the work is to take place.

Find some soil fairly free of rocks and debris for the shelf around the fish. Add enough water to the soil so that it will remain where placed (Fig. 26). A

Figure 26. A tarpon in the Florida Keys is being molded. A base or shelf of sand is built up around the fish to the midline of the body. The exposed side of the tarpon is the "show side."

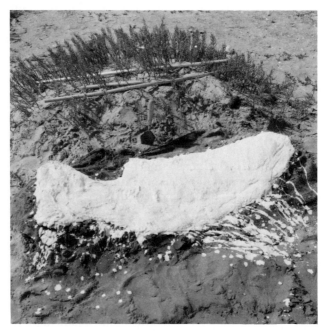

Figure 27. A layer of plaster and then sisal and plaster are applied as in Figs. 9 to 11.

Figure 28. The mold is reinforced with thin wall conduit or other pipe.

Figure 29. When the plaster has set, the mold is turned over (with the fish in it); the second half of the mold is made in the same manner as the first.

25

Figure 30. A close-up of the "show side" of the mold.

Figure 31. Clean the edges of the molds; wire the two halves together so that the insides won't get damaged.

seashore beach is an excellent spot for this type of work. Plenty of salt water is at hand to mix with the sand, and the plaster bowls can be cleaned easily in the surf. Remember, though, that fresh water is still necessary for mixing the plaster.

The advantage of working outdoors is that the plaster bowls can be cleaned without fuss, and any excess plaster can be dumped on a pile. And, of course, there is no worry of decorating the floor, walls, or furniture with plaster. The actual molding of the fish is followed in the same manner as described above in this section.

If the mold is to be transported some distance, it is advisable to add sisal for strength. Dip a handful of this fiber in plaster and place it over the first coat of plaster until the entire fish and shelf are covered. An added precaution is the placement of pipe along the sides and across the mold (Fig. 28). For further details read Chapter 13.

MOLDING AT HOME.   Although more care has to be exercised while working with plaster at home or in the laboratory, there are many advantages of convenience which cannot be had in the field. Fresh water is at hand, the sun cannot dry out the specimen, and wind cannot blow sand over it.

A frozen specimen must first be thawed out. If the fins are dry, do not attempt to place them in position until they have been soaked in water. Wrap wet cloths or wet paper towels around the fins and the tail, or place the entire fish in water. When the fins are soft, prepare the fish as previously described.

If you have been able to bring home only the skin, proceed as follows to build the body out to its former contours for molding. Fill the head and skin with ground gray asbestos which has been mixed with water to a puttylike consistency. See "Asbestos" in Chapter 15. Sew the skin together partially; then add or remove asbestos. Finish sewing the skin, turn the fish over carefully, and proceed to model the fish to its original proportions. Use the outline tracing and photos of the fresh fish.

Either of two methods can be used to mold a fish indoors—choice is a matter of personal preference. One way is to build a temporary, shallow, rectangular box, about the height of a mold. Grease the inside of the box or line it with wax paper so that the set plaster will not adhere to the wood. Pour the plaster into the receptacle until it reaches halfway up the sides of the box. Place the fish on the plaster carefully. Press the specimen here and there into the plaster until the plaster is forced to the midline of the fish's back and the midline of the belly. Be careful not to allow plaster to flow over the faceup side of the fins and tail; if it does, the plaster can be scraped away when it starts to set. As the plaster begins to harden, cut some round conelike keys along the sides or the shelf of the mold. After the plaster has set, apply the separator and pour the other side. Pour the plaster slowly, starting at one end, and be careful not to lock in air pockets with plaster.

The other way of molding indoors is to construct a shelf around the fish the same way as when working in the field. Instead of sand or soil, however, use asbestos—a clean, pleasant material which can be worked many times over and over again. I use ground gray asbestos that is inexpensive. A 50-pound bag will be sufficient for any trout, bass, or bluefish. Mix the asbestos with water until it reaches a smooth consistency and can be troweled. Do not mix too much water with the asbestos or it will not stay put. Place the asbestos in a bowl, and add water to it gradually while mixing it by hand. With a little practice the asbetos can be shaped perfectly around the fish (Fig. 7). When finished with the job, dump the wet asbestos in a 5-gallon pail that has a cover. If the asbestos has dried after being stored away for a few months, simply add water, let it soak a while, and then work the asbestos with both hands until it becomes soft.

With a bit of care plaster can be used at home in the basement or workroom without making a mess. A piece of glass on the table top facilitates neat work. Rub some grease over the glass so that the plaster scrapes up easily. Layers of newspapers can be used or a table top can be greased. Have a waste bucket handy to accommodate whatever plaster is left over in the mixing bowl. If the plaster receptacles are to be cleaned in the sink, be sure to remove as much plaster as possible first. Then, run some water into the bowl and work the sides well with a scrub brush or some rough material such as excelsior or steel wool. During this process be sure the tap water is going, otherwise the plaster sediment may accumulate in the sink trap and stop up the drain system. I have been cleaning plaster bowls in sinks for many years and have yet to incur any trouble with drainage of the sinks. However, the plaster bowl can be cleaned in a tub of water. Later, pour off the water; the plaster remaining in the bottom of the tub will not harden and may be disposed of outdoors in the trash can.

CHAPTER THREE

Rubber Molds

The rubber mold has only one disadvantage compared to a plaster mold: it is more expensive if only one cast is desired. It does, however, have several advantages. The fluid rubber can be applied directly over the specimen after the fish slime is washed or wiped off. The rubber captures the definition of the scales in extraordinary detail. This kind of mold requires no application of a separator before the polyester resin is troweled in to make a cast, and any number of casts can be obtained from one mold.

The fish is prepared for molding in the same manner as described in Chapter 2 (Fig. 7). In addition, a retaining wall or an edge built about an inch above the sand or asbestos shelf will contain the rubber within the confines of the intended mold. Note that the pectoral and the two ventral fins can be molded in the same operation as the rest of the fish. Position the fins on the shelf around the fish and press them gently into the sand or asbestos.

Mix the rubber and hardener as prescribed on the label of the container; flow it over the fish and the shelf to a depth of about ¼ inch. A rubber mold of such thickness is highly flexible, so a supporting layer of plaster is built over the rubber after it has set. If the plaster casing is large, it should be reinforced with sisal or strengthened with conduit pipe. Polyester resin can be used instead of plaster for the casing; it is lighter and much sturdier. A couple of pieces of conduit pipe secured along the length of the casing will be an advantage in handling and storing the mold. When the first half of the mold is completed, including rubber and supporting casing, turn the mold and the fish over; clean away any sand or asbestos clinging to the fish and the rubber shelf of the mold. Repeat the operation performed on the other half of the mold, including rubber and casing. Before mixing the rubber, however, brush the shelf of the first half of the rubber mold with a coat of shellac to prevent the fresh, fluid rubber from sticking to it.

CASTING IN A RUBBER MOLD. As stated previously, the rubber mold does not require a separator before the polyester resin is applied. Trowel a

Figure 32. Rubber molds, such as this one of a largemouth bass, capture extraordinary detail. Many casts can be reproduced from a single mold. Note that the pectoral and ventral fins are included in the mold (on the shelf) and will be cast together with the polyester resin body of the bass.

thin coat of resin to both sides of the mold, including over the dorsal, anal, and tail fins. A light filler such as whiting or Cab-o-sil (fumed silica) should be mixed into the resin to prevent it from sliding down the sides of the mold. When that has set, trowel in a second coat. Place a thin layer of fiberglass (glass cloth) over the fins for strength. Then wipe a bit of resin over them. Anchor a piece of wood into the cast by pressing it lightly into

Figure 33. A rubber mold is very flexible and must be supported by a casing of plaster or, as shown, polyester resin which is much lighter. Electrical conduit (pipe) is attached to the casing for stability and easier handling when storing.

the resin. The wood will serve as a base into which screws can be inserted, if the mount is to be secured to a plaque or some natural base, such as a weathered stump. Touch the edges of the cast lightly with resin.

Apply the same resin to both sides of the fins which have been impressed in the rubber on the shelf. Now position the halves against each other and squeeze them together with large clamps. The job is done. When the resin has set, open the mold, remove the cast and finish it as described in the section "Cleaning and Finishing the Cast" in Chapter 4.

When storing the mold always secure the halves to each other with wire. In this way, the rubber will not bend out of shape and will be protected by its casings from damage.

CHAPTER FOUR

Casts

The cast or mount is reproduced from the plaster mold. Fishes can be cast satisfactorily in four mediums: plaster of Paris, wax, casting compound, and synthetic or plastic materials. I do not advise the use of latex or other rubberlike substances for mounts or casts that are to be permanent. Within a few years the rubber hardens and cracks, and the paint begins to peel.

PREPARING THE MOLD FOR CASTING

If one side of the mold was cracked or otherwise damaged so that it is no longer one rigid piece, repair it in this manner. Place the two halves together with the damaged side facing up. Check to see that the halves fit snugly. Sponge water onto the area around the crack or cracks. This is necessary—otherwise the dry mold will suck moisture from the new plaster and results will be unsatisfactory. Mix a pan of plaster and dip in pieces of tow, sisal fiber, or excelsior. Apply these hunks of plaster-fiber liberally over the cracked or broken surface. Do not disturb the mold until the plaster used in repair is completely set. Of course, a one-piece mold can be repaired by using the same techniques.

Usually, a one-piece mold is used for casting fishes in plaster. Wax casts can be reproduced from a one- or two-piece mold, depending on where and how the mounts are to be displayed. Casts in compound or in plastics require a two-piece mold to reproduce a whole fish.

All molds require attention and preparation, however, before the casting medium can be applied. The mold should be thoroughly dry. If sand or asbestos has been used for the shelf in producing the mold, all bits of loose material should be gently swept out of the hollow impression by using a 2-inch paint brush. The shelves of the mold can be swept with a scrubbing brush.

32

Figure 34. A steelhead with eye inserted before painting the cast.

Figure 35. Cast of a tarpon. The next step is to saw off the areas around the fin.

Figure 36. Cast of a brown trout ready for painting.

Figure 37. Cast of a Nassau Grouper. The next step is to drill out holes to accommodate the fins.

SHOW SIDE OF MOLD. The show side of the mold is the half that will reproduce the show side of the fish. If the mold is intended for reproducing a mount in plastic or casting compound, give it a preliminary thin coat of shellac. This preliminary coat will make it easier to detect small holes or pockets caused by air bubbles, foreign material, or damage. Fill these defects with modeling clay or small pieces of wax. If necessary, model the repaired surface with an appropriate tool. Sometimes the detail of the lips or parts of the head in the mold is broken when removing the original fish from the mold. Now is the time to model in any detail that might have been snapped off.

Apply another coat of shellac, thinned 50-50 with alcohol, to the mold. When this has dried, apply yet another coat. Several brushings of shellac will be required until the mold begins to acquire a gloss. The next step is to apply the separator—either formula 6 (see Chapter 15) or furniture polish wax out of a spray can. The show side of the mold is now ready for casting.

REAR HALF OF MOLD. In a two-piece mold the rear half reproduces the back portion of the fish, the side that goes against the wall. With a soft pencil or crayon, outline the areas of the mold that are to be sawed off or chipped away (Fig. 38). In the illustration the line just before the tail indicates where the mold is sawed off complete. The oblong-shaped outline is a guide to the area to be sawed from this side of the mold. Use a key-hole saw. Drill holes in the four corners with a countersink tool to accommodate the saw (Fig. 39).

The lines around the dorsal and anal fins—about an inch beyond the edge of the impression of the fin—indicates the areas that are chipped away to a depth of about ½ inch. The reason for removing these areas is to accommodate the cast fins which have to be thicker than the originals. There must be room for them when the mold halves are placed together; otherwise, the halves of the mold will not fit snugly. The entire process is demonstrated in Figs. 38 to 43.

Shellac the mold and apply separator in the same way as for the show side. Further treatment of the molds for the individual methods is included in the following sections.

CASTS IN PLASTER

The easiest, quickest, and least expensive method of producing a cast is to do it in plaster (molding plaster No. 1). Only a one-side mold is necessary, and no preliminary coat of shellac is needed. The cast can be made into a medallion type, which includes a plaque cast as one piece with the fish; or the plaque can be eliminated. Let us consider the medallion type first. Place the mold in a pan of water (if the mold is too large, run water over it)

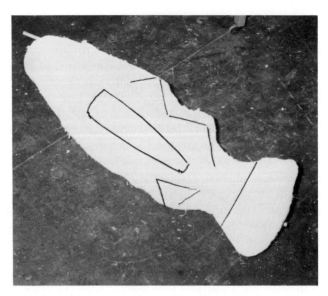

Figure 38. Outline the areas of the mold to be sawed off or chipped away.

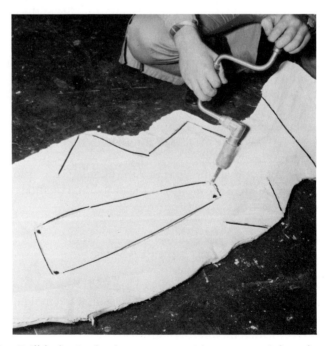

Figure 39. Drill holes in the four corners with a countersink tool to accommodate the saw.

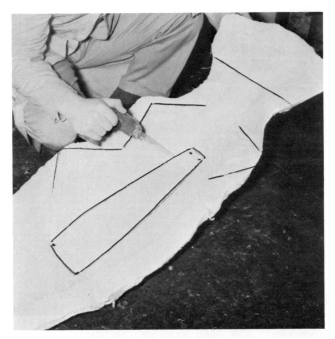

Figure 40. Use a key-hole saw.

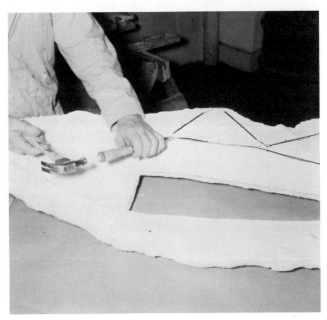

Figure 41. Chip away the fin areas to a depth of about ½ inch.

37

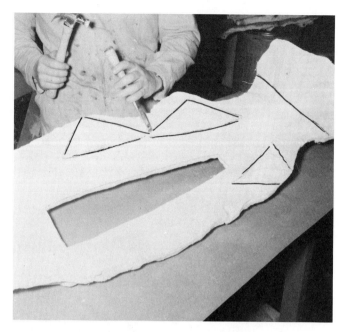

Figure 42. Chip away around the dorsal and anal fins—about an inch beyond the edge of the impression of the fin.

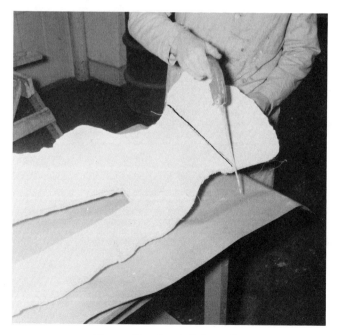

Figure 43. Saw off the tail.

38

until it is thoroughly wet. This requires only a few minutes. (A saturated mold will not draw moisture from the fresh plaster of the cast, and saturation helps in eliminating bubble holes in the cast.) Remove the mold from the water when air bubbles are no longer released from the plaster. Get rid of any drops of water in the mold with a paper towel or a cloth. Apply the sterine separator to the entire mold, including the shelf. Rub your fingers gently over the mold to smooth out any sterine that might have been applied to excess.

Flow the plaster into the hollow of the mold, starting at one end. Let the hollow fill first; then allow the plaster to run onto the shelf of the mold. Wait until the plaster starts setting and reaches a heavy whipped-cream consistency. Trowel enough plaster over all until a thickness of about ¾ inch is evident on the shelf of the mold. In other words, the plaque will be constructed of plaster ¾ inch thick. If the fish is more than 14-16 inches in length, the plaque can be reinforced with tow or sisal dipped in plaster. Insert two pieces of looped wire into the back of the cast while the plaster is still soft. Turn the ends so that the wire will not pull out. These loops will serve as eye-hooks to hold a wire for hanging purposes. Another method is to insert a looped wire into the center of the top edge of the plaque.

Run a trowel or a knife along the edge of the cast before the plaster is set. It is easier to obtain a clean, smooth edge in this manner than to hack away at the hard cast when it is removed from the mold.

A mold that is to be used for a plaster cast should be made thin and without sisal or tow reinforcements so that it can be chipped away easily. A small ¼-inch chisel and a light hammer should be used. The addition of color, such as bluing, to the water when mixing plaster for either the mold or the cast will be a help in differentiating one from the other during the chipping process. Damage to the cast, by the chisel biting too deeply, will

Figure 44.   Sturgeon cast in plaster.

Figure 45. Mako shark cast in plaster.

be reduced because it can be clearly seen where the mold stops and the cast begins.

The pectoral and ventral fins can be reproduced separately in plaster, but I do not advise it; plaster fins, extending outward from the body, are too fragile. It is preferable to replace these fins with artificial ones carved (a small electrical grinding tool is best) from sheet celluloid, Plexiglas or other plasticlike material. For this method, cut the original fins from the body before molding; then trace their outline onto the celluloid with a sharp tool and cut them out. A simpler method is to fold the fins against the body, therefore including them in the mold. In other words, the pectoral and ventral fins can be reproduced in plaster just as they appeared folded against the body.

If the cast is to appear as a whole fish, without a back or plaque, avoid flowing the plaster onto the shelf of the mold except in the areas containing the impressions of the tail and fins. When the plaster starts to thicken, trowel more of it over the cast—about ¾ inch over the body and about ½ inch over the tail and dorsal and anal fins. Insert wires into the back of the fish as described previously. Or the cast can be placed directly against the wall (no space between wall and fish) by eliminating the wires. Instead, carve out a hole in the back of the cast and insert a piece of metal or wire across the top end of the hole while the plaster is still soft. With this method the fish plaque can be placed on a nail or hook snug against the wall.

When the cast has been separated from the mold, carve out the eye area to the proper depth to receive the glass eye with room to spare. Brush shellac into the hollow. When the shellac dries run some hot wax into the hole and then insert the glass eye. Smooth the wax around the eye with a tool. An easy way of applying the wax is to heat any small metal tool and touch it to a piece of beeswax held directly over the eye impression. Let the wax drop into it.

Now check over the cast and fill in any defects with plaster or wax; if plaster is used, first wet the area to be repaired. Scrape away any irregularities in the plaque. Chisel or cut away any bits of plaster that may be attached to the fish. The lips, jaws, and gill cover may require deeper lines; cut them in with a knife or other pointed instrument.

If the fish has been cast without the plaque, bevel the edges of the body and fins from their outer edge inward toward the back of the fish. In this way the fish will appear to be fully cast when hung upon the wall.

Cover the dried cast with shellac thinned 50-50 with commercial alcohol and apply several coats until the cast begins to hint of gloss. Paint the fish (see Chapter 6).

CASTS IN WAX

The wax cast is another method of casting fish that may be accomplished easily at home and with minimal expense. In certain instances casting in wax is superior to any other means of constructing models of fishes. It is the simplest and fastest method of obtaining many reproductions out of the same mold. For example, in museum display groups, a school of fish that usually travel with age-mates of the same size can all be produced from the same mold. It is a simple matter to warm the individual casts in hot water so that their bodies can be turned here and there to make them look slightly different from one another. Wax fish can be cast in a half mold, which is usually sufficient when constructing a school of fish where only one side will be seen, or a whole fish can be cast using a two-piece mold. A wax cast is not fragile, nor is it a messy job if done properly.

WAX CASTS—HALF MOLD. Let us assume first that only the show side of the fish will be cast. Immerse the mold in hot water. If the mold is too large for a tub or the sink, pour hot water over it. The mold should be soaked at least until all the air bubbles are released from it. In other words, the mold should absorb all the water it can.

A separating medium is required between the plaster mold and the wax cast, as it is necessary in all casting processes. However, a different, simple separator is used. Before applying wax to the mold, soap it well with a thin solution of green surgical soap or shaving soap; or the usual soap powder or soap flakes used in the kitchen may be brushed dry onto the wet mold until a heavy lather forms. Remove the lather with a brush. Run the brush over the mold and wipe it on a cloth or towel after every few strokes. Sweep the brush over the mold until a slight polished effect is obtained. A thin film of soap will be left on the surface of the mold which will facilitate the separation of the wax cast from the plaster mold. If the wax is too hot when applied to the mold, however, there will be difficulty in separating the two. I have found that oil, Vaseline, and lard, for example, are not satisfactory separators.

A fish reproduced in wax can be made as durable as plaster if it is handled with care. But any wax used in an unadulterated form in casting is unsatisfactory because either it is too brittle or the melting point is low. It is difficult to work a cast that is brittle; and it would be embarrassing if on a hot summer's day, while you are proudly displaying a wax-cast trophy to a friend, the fish's jaws begin to droop and its tail begins to sag. Therefore, a small portion of another type of wax, such as carnauba, is added to inexpensive paraffin wax. The carnauba wax brings the composition to a higher melting point. A shop that carries art supplies can advise you regarding proper waxes for casting.

Other qualities desirable in a wax casting compound are toughness, bending without breaking, and no warping or cracking. Common rosin, which is the resin of a pine tree and often called colophony, added to the wax in a correct amount does the job. It also causes the composition to harden more slowly and thus, to a great extent, prevents cracking. For the correct preparation of this casting wax, see the section on formulas (Chapter 15).

Anyone interested in using wax as a casting medium may come across many different formulas. The individual formulas may be composed of different types of wax—all of which have about the same melting point. The addition of several kinds of wax only complicates the matter and means nothing. Many who work with wax add substances such as whiting, talc, and plaster of Paris to the wax. Why? I don't know. These substances only act as fillers and accomplish nothing except to change the color of the composition. Also, when a filler such as whiting is added in excess, the resulting composition becomes brittle and may even crumble. Stay with the simple formula found in Chapter 15. Fillers are justified only when certain effects such as metal, stone, and wood are desired. The angler may find it interesting to experiment by adding powdered glass, marble meal, or metallic powders such as copper, silver, or gold.

Two methods can be used in applying the wax composition to the mold—brushing or pouring. If the mold is fairly small and has been heated in hot water, pouring wax into the mold is satisfactory. Brushing the wax into the mold, however, has many advantages. The mold does not have to be lifted and tilted back and forth in order to place the wax in the same thickness over the entire mold. There is less chance of border lines forming as the wax cools during the process of tilting the mold. It is more economical because there is no loss of wax over the sides, and the cast is of uniform thickness throughout.

As soon as the mold is taken out of the hot water, apply the soap quickly so that the mold remains warm during the application of wax. No drops of water should be in the mold; dab them out with a piece of cotton. Now pour or brush in the hot wax. If pouring, tilt the mold from side to side so that the wax reaches all parts and crevices. Pour excess wax back into the pot. Repeat the process immediately, and repeat again until the cast has attained a thickness of about ⅛ to ¼ inch. Before removing the cast from the mold, it should be reinforced with two or three layers of gauze that have first been dipped in the pot of wax. (Include the tail and fins in the reinforcement process unless the wax fins will be replaced with fins constructed out of Celluloid or other plastic material.) Brush more wax onto the gauze until it is well impregnated with wax. Be sure the wax is hot enough to penetrate the gauze completely so that it will stick to the surface beneath the gauze. Otherwise, the gauze will act to separate the two layers of wax.

Absorbent cotton can be used instead of the gauze. Spread a thin layer of cotton over the entire cast including fins and tail, and then brush the wax over the cotton. If the cast needs to be strengthened even more, this can be accomplished by applying plaster of Paris. Dip gauze, tow, strips of loose burlap, or other fibrous material into the plaster and apply it to the cast.

If brushing wax into the mold (the better method) instead of pouring, use a small varnish brush. Of course, bring the pot of wax to the mold so that the brush can be dipped quickly from the pot to the mold. Reinforce the brushed cast the same way as the poured cast.

As a base for inserting screw eyes or hooks for hanging purposes, place a piece of wood in back of the cast and anchor it with cotton dipped in hot wax. A couple of nails tapped into the sides of the wood so that their heads protrude about an inch will provide good spots to attach the cotton. The cotton can be placed in position dry, and then the wax can be applied with a brush. If you intend to immerse the mold in hot water to facilitate the removal of the wax cast, the wood should be waterproofed with hot wax before securing it in the cast.

When brushing the wax into the mold, extend the wax over the edge of the hollow impression of the mold and beyond the edges of the fins and tail for about ½ inch. This will facilitate removal of the cast from the mold by supplying an area to pry under without damage to the cast. Sometimes, especially if there are undercuts in the plaster mold, the cast will not separate easily. In this case, the mold can be warmed just enough to bend the wax slightly, here and there, so that it can be removed from the mold without damage. Then the fish should be pressed back into shape before the wax cools completely.

Upon the removal of the cast, or positive form, from the mold, tiny defects in the structure, usually caused by gas bubbles, may be apparent. The defects and any other blemishes can be corrected by filling in these areas with a pastelike mixture made in the following manner. Pour a small amount of the wax composition into a glass jar with a screw-on top. Add a few drops of turpentine to the melted wax. This will bring down the melting point of the wax and make it pliable after setting. Place the top on the jar. Shake it well until the wax and the turpentine are mixed. Before using this paste, place the jar in warm water to soften the contents. Use a sculptor's wooden tool, or any other similar device, to apply and model the paste onto the cast. Eventually, the turpentine evaporates, and the repaired area is as hard as the rest of the cast. The repaired areas should have a day or two to dry and harden.

It is not necessary to use the wax composition for repairs if a job must be done in a hurry. Regular putty can be substituted, although the repair job will not be as good. The putty can be colored to match the rest of the cast—if that is desired—by adding pigment (oil color) just as it comes out of the tube. If this makes the putty too sticky, add some whiting or dry plaster of Paris.

If the fish is to be painted with oil or lacquer colors, a thin coat of shellac (thinned 50-50 with alcohol) should be applied first. Otherwise, the surface of the cast may soften from contact with the oil, turpentine, or lacquer medium in the paint. The best substance to use for shellacking is the clear yellow liquid that rises to the surface of a jar of white shellac when it has been left standing. This light yellow liquid should be diluted with three parts alcohol before using.

WAX CASTS—FULL MOLD. If the whole fish is to be cast (rather than one side), a two-piece mold is used. Cut an oblong section out of the back side of the mold and saw off the tail section as directed earlier. Proceed to brush in the wax and reinforcements as described previously. Remove the casts from both sides of the mold. With tools such as knives, mounted razor blades, scalpels, or woodcarver chisels, trim the edges of the casts which overlapped the edges of the molds. Trim the halves so that they fit together perfectly. One method of cementing two pieces of a wax cast together is to heat a knife blade over a flame and then draw it between the two pieces. The wax on both edges will melt, and as the wax cools the edges will bind. The two pieces must be pressed together firmly while the knife is being drawn between them. Also, they should be held together long enough afterward to allow the wax to cool and thus set. Another way is to trim the edges of the halves, place them together, and then apply a hot tool in a few spots inside so that the two pieces are held in place. Then clinch the halves together permanently by applying cotton dipped in hot wax to the seam. Gauze dipped in hot wax can be used also. Brush more wax over the seam area if necessary. If the fish cast is to be screwed to a plaque, place a piece of wood in the cast and secure it with cotton and hot wax.

A wax cast of a fish can be bent into a different position by placing it in a pan of warm water. Do not rush the job because the cast cracks easily if it has not warmed enough. If a fin or tail is to be curved, it is not necessary to immerse the entire cast.

FINS. If a more realistic cast is desired, *all fins* can be cut from the wax cast body of the fish and replaced with fins carved out of Celluloid or other plasticlike material available in sheet form. Another method is to mold the fins and cast them in plastic (see Fins in the latter part of this chapter). In either case it is necessary to carve holes in the wax body to receive the artificial fins. When producing the fins, leave enough material at their bases for anchoring with the wax body. Insert the fins, place in position, and anchor them from behind the wax cast with cotton and hot wax. Finish anchoring one fin before starting on another. An additional coat of wax will be necessary at the base of the fins on the show side of the fish. Do this carefully with a ¼- or ½-inch brush. Then model for correct anatomy by scraping or adding wax as needed. The areas where the fins were inserted can be made smooth by going over them with a piece of cloth dipped in turpentine.

CASTS IN COMPOUND

Before plastics were developed commercially to a point where they could be poured or spread in a mold and set without oven treatment at high temperatures, I cast fish in a compound or composition material which proved satisfactory in producing fairly strong and durable mounts. The composition that is referred to as casting compound in this book is a mixture of asbestos, dextrin, whiting, glycerin, molding plaster, and a touch of carbolic acid. (The formula and the directions for preparing this compound are found in Chapter 15). Casting in compound requires much more time than casting in plastics (next section), and it is more complicated. The materials that form the compound, however, are inexpensive in comparison to plastics.

The entire fish, including pectoral and ventral fins (if they are folded against the body while molding), can be cast in this pastelike medium. If the pectoral fin is to be extended away from the body, it can be cast in plastic or cut and carved out of a sheet of Celluloid. All the fins can be carved, if so desired, out of any type of sheet plasticlike material. The tail can be replaced also, but I advise against this because it is practically impossible to retain the natural contours of the body where it meets the tail.

Figure 46.   King salmon produced in casting compound.

Select the side of the mold that is to reproduce the show side of the fish.
Cut the oblong piece of plaster out of the other half of the mold, saw off the
tail, and chip out the fin areas as described previously (Figs. 38 to 43).
Shellac the mold (thinned 50-50 with alcohol) until a sheen is evident.
Apply the wax-kerosene separator (formula 6 in Chapter 15).

Mix the casting compound with water and molding plaster. Trowel the
first layer into both sides of the mold, to a depth of ⅛ inch. Then cut strips of
cheesecloth that will fit conveniently into the cast. These strips should be
1-2 inches wide and about 4-8 inches long, depending on the size of the fish.
Press compound into these strips with a putty knife, using enough force so
that the material is well impregnated. It is best to do this on a piece of glass
that has been greased. Turn the strips over and apply them to the mold so

Figure 47.   Alaskan sheefish produced in casting compound.

that they meet or overlap each other a bit. Cover the entire area of both molds. Rub more compound over the cheesecloth layer after it has been placed in the mold and before applying the next course. In small fishes two layers of material may be sufficient, though, as many layers as desired may be worked into the cast. Allow one layer of reinforcement to set before placing the next one; otherwise, the cast will require an unnecessarily long time to dry. Be sure to add water and plaster to the casting compounds because this facilitates the setting of the compound. For certain purposes I have reinforced the cast with ⅛-inch mesh wire. Large fish can be strengthened with ¼-inch mesh wire. Cut the mesh wire into strips, place them lengthwise into the cast, and secure them with compound.

After the compound has set, trim the cast in both halves of the mold where the edge of the cast meets the edge of the shelf. Place the halves together and check to see that they fit snugly. If they don't, notice the spots that are responsible and trim away a bit more of the cast. When you are satisfied that the halves fit well, tie wire around each end of the mold so the halves cannot be jarred from position. Now reach inside the cast and dampen, with a sponge and water, the area along the seams where the two halves of the cast meet. With a narrow spatula press compound (mixed with plaster and water) along the seams. Then cut a few narrow lengths (an inch or two wide depending on the size of the fish) of cheesecloth into which casting compound has been pressed. Insert these strips along the seams and bind them thoroughly to the cast with more compound.

Place the mold containing the cast over a radiator or in a warm room for faster drying. If the cast is not thoroughly dried when removing the mold, parts of the surface of the cast will remain in the mold and thus your fish will be ruined. To be certain no damage will occur to the show side, remove the back side of the mold first, when it is set and dry. The back side will usually be ready to come clear first. Then leave the fish in the show side of the mold for another day or two in the drying room—to make doubly sure that the cast is dried thoroughly. Then chip away, with a small hammer and chisel, around the edges of the mold holding the cast. This procedure will facilitate release of the cast from the mold.

If slight defects or air pockets appear in the cast, repair them with compound mixed liberally with plaster and water; or plaster alone mixed with water can be used.

Trim the body, fins, and tail, and treat them lightly with fine sandpaper. It will be necessary to add casting compound along the outside of the seam where the two parts of the cast come together; allow to set, then trim and smooth with fine sandpaper.

Drill holes through the cast where the fins are to be located. Insert the bases of the artificial fins and secure them from the inside with the compound. It may be necessary to support the fins in position while the

Figure 48. This gar, 3 feet in length, was reproduced entirely in polyester resin excepting the original snout.

Figure 49. The original snout, preserved in Formalin, is attached to the polyester resin head. The line where they meet is impossible to discern.

compound is setting. Modeling clay may be used for this purpose. Also, it may be wise not to place all the fins at once. In other words, it is less awkward to place a fin or two and wait until they have set in position before working on the others.

When the entire fish has dried thoroughly, apply a coat or two of shellac (thinned 50-50 with alcohol) to every part of the fish, including the back side.

Figure 50.   The polyester resin mount of a 23 inch rainbow trout is displayed without a panel against the wall. The arrangement is simple: a nail is driven into the wall and a hole appropriately drilled into the back side of the mount at a slight angle holds the fish in position.

Set the eye (see latter part of this chapter) and paint the fish (Chapter 6). Apply a coat or two of clear varnish to every part of the fish. If the fish is to be placed on a plaque, insert a block of wood as described earlier.

CASTS IN PLASTICS OR RESINS

It is my considered opinion that the advent of easily obtainable, durable, plastic materials that can be cast in plaster molds without requiring intense heat has been the most important contribution ever made to the art of creating likelike replicas of fishes for museum displays or trophies for sport fishermen. By far the best plastic available to date is polyester resin, a popular item for repairing boats. It is available in paint shops and hardware stores, as well as through boat supply dealers. It is a liquid that will set in less than half an hour when properly mixed with a few drops of hardener. When set, through its natural chemical action at room temperature, it becomes a hard material that will not shrink or change its form, nor will it be affected by weather changes. Furthermore, it will never crack, peel ooze grease, or appear wizened, as do most skin mounts. Actually, it is indestructible, unless, of course, the mount is dropped onto a hard surface and a fin is chipped or broken off. Even then, another fin can be cast in the

Figure 51. This replica of a 1560-pound black marlin, the largest game fish ever taken on rod and reel, was presented to the Smithsonian Institution, Museum of Natural History by Alfred C. Glassell, Jr., who caught the fish off Cabo Blanco, Peru, on August 4, 1953.

The mount is a composite of taxidermic procedures. The bill, parts of the head, pectoral fins, tail, and most of the body skin are the only remains of the original fish. The dorsal fin is plywood; the second dorsal fin, first and second anal fins and the antennalike ventrals located beneath the pectorals have been reproduced in metal.

Figure 52.   The author, using rod and reel, collected this arapaima or pirarucu in the Rupununi, a jungle river in Guyana, South America. His native assistant, a Macusi Indian, stands by the specimen. The arapaima is the world's largest strictly fresh water fish.

Figure 53. The polyester resin cast of the same arapaima now rests in an exhibit case in Yale's Peabody Museum of Natural History.

Figure 54. Imaginative wall mounts are far superior to the usual "all alike" wooden panels that always appear as if straight from the carpenter's shop.

same material to replace the damaged one without the slightest change in appearance.

All of the most recently published taxidermy books that I have reviewed recommend the use of the polyester resin method only for certain "oily fish" and only fish of a certain size. That is nonsense. There is not a fish that swims that cannot be reproduced to advantage in polyester resin, and that includes specimens of all sizes from a minnow to a whale shark. Some books dealing with general taxidermy give only suggestions regarding the creation of polyester resin fishes. Others treat the subject sparingly or

Figure 55. The first step in casting a plastic is to apply the wax-kerosene separator. (Clear lacquer or spray furniture wax polish may be used.)

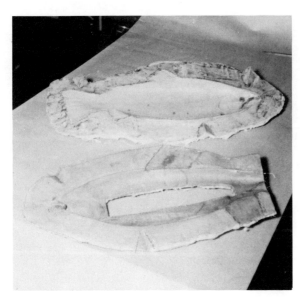

Figure 56. Apply the separator to both halves of the mold.

Figure 57. Apply the plastic (polyester resin) with a spatula.

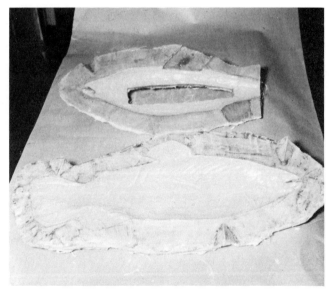

Figure 58. Both halves as they appear with one coat of plastic.

Figure 59. The second or reinforcing layer is applied after the first coat of plastic has set. This mixture appears black in the photo because it has asbestos mixed into it.

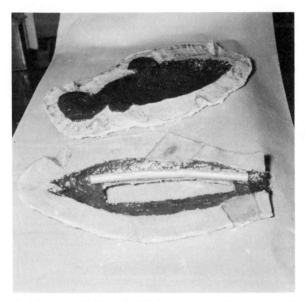

Figure 60. Both sides are reinforced with this mixture. If necessary, the wall side of the cast could be reinforced with a piece of conduit pipe as shown. The pipe is attached to the cast with plastic.

Figure 61. When securing the halves of the cast together in larger fish, place narrow strips of woven glass over the seam after the second application of plastic. The other half of the mold goes over this. More plastic is applied from the inside, along the strips of glass cloth—thus binding them to the cast.

Figure 62. The first step in removing the cast from the mold is to chip away any plastic that may have flowed over the edge of the back opening of the mold.

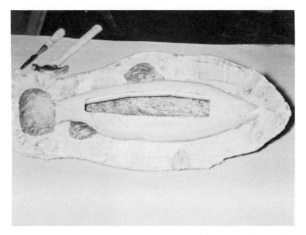

Figure 63. Separate the halves of the mold by inserting a chisel between them. The cast will remain in one side.

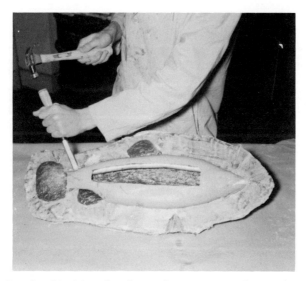

Figure 64. Tap the chisel into the plaster about ¼ to ½ inch away from the cast at the caudal peduncle.

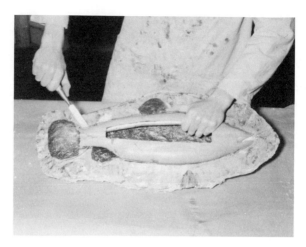

Figure 65. Apply downward pressure on the chisel and the cast should come out.

Figure 66. The cast of the brown trout as it appears when removed from the mold.

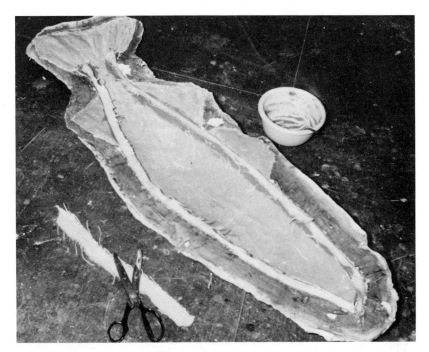

Figure 67. Medium and large fish require stronger casts. This is accomplished by backing the first layer of plastic with glass cloth (woven glass) and an additional layer of plastic.

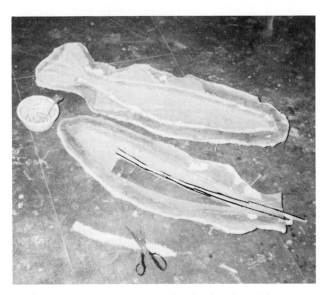

Figure 68. Conduit pipe should be secured to both sides of the opening of the wall side of the large fish.

incompletely, with pitfalls for the would-be or inexperienced taxidermist. In this section I attempt to present the subject updated, in detail, and in its entirety.

When the plaster mold has dried and the coats of shellac have also dried, the separator or mold release is applied as directed in the earlier section, "Preparing the Mold for Casting." Although the shellac and rubbed-in wax-vaseline-kerosene separator is my favorite mold release, a simpler and faster method can be used. Handy, easy-to-use spray cans of clear lacquer, acrylic, and enamel may be obtained in any paint store. Lacquer dries the fastest and the hardest of the three. Spray light coats into the mold and along its shelf until no spot is left uncovered. Ordinary spray wax used as furniture polish also does the job. When dry, the wax may need some working over with a soft brush to eliminate areas of excessive application that may cover scale definition.

APPLYING PLASTIC. Read the instructions carefully before mixing a batch of polyester resin. It is especially important to add the exact amount (usually in drops) of hardener to the base liquid. If too much hardener is used the material will set too quickly; if not enough is added the setting will be delayed.

The polyester resin is much too fluid to apply "as is" onto the mold; therefore it is necessary to give it some body by adding a substance that will not oppose the action of the plastic mixture. Various kinds of so-called "fillers" are available from taxidermy supply dealers, art supply stores and other commercial establishments dealing with casting compounds used by sculptors. For example, one of the best fillers is fumed silica that is sold under various trade names such as Cab-o-sil (see Chapter 15). Powdered whiting is inexpensive and works well with plastic, although it is not easily obtainable in rural areas. It is wise for anyone not experienced in mixing plastic and fillers to experiment with a small amount of each material. Just enough filler should be added so the mixture will stay where spread on the side of the mold. The object is to thicken the plastic so that it does not run down into the center of the plaster mold. On the other hand, if too much filler is in the mixture, it will weaken the polyester resin and have a tendency to crumble when set.

Apply the plastic with a limber spatula. Take care not to press the tool with force, otherwise the mold may be marked. Do not apply the casting mixture above the impression of the fish, that is, onto the shelf of the mold. Do, however, spread it to include about ½ inch below the margins of the tail and fins on the show side of the mold. Spread the material carefully in a thin layer over the entire impression of the fish. The other half of the mold (which will be the back side of the fish) does not require the application of the casting substance over the fin areas (obviously, they have been chipped away) because space is needed to accommodate the cast fins, which are slightly thicker than the original fins.

Within a couple hours, the first coat should be set enough (even if not completely hard to the touch) to receive the second or reinforcing layer (Fig. 59). A heavier proportion of any filler used in the first coat will work as well. I prefer ground asbestos because it is inexpensive, and when mixed with the plastic, the mixture stays where it is applied. I do not recommend that asbestos be used in the first coat of plastic because it is a much rougher substance than whiting or one of the other packaged fillers. Although small- and medium-sized fishes do not require glass cloth to strengthen the cast, some workers prefer to use it as the reinforcing agent, rather than a heavier mixture of plastic.

ANOTHER METHOD OF OBTAINING A POLYESTER RESIN CAST. Apply a coat of polyester resin to both sides of the mold, including the dorsal, anal, and tail fins (thinly over the fins). When that has set trowel in a second, heavier coat, again over the entire fish, but not onto the shelf. Place a layer of thin fiberglass over the fin impressinos (to strengthen the fins) and wipe a bit of resin over them. Anchor a piece of wood into the side of the cast that is not the show side to serve as a support to receive the screws attaching the plaque to the mount. Dab some resin along hte eges of the cast in both halves of the mold. Be sure that the shelves of the mold are well covered with a separator. Fit the halves to each other and squeeze them together as much as possible by use of large clamps. Leave the clamps in place until the polyester resin has set. Stout elastic bands may be used instead of clamps.

STRENGTHENING THE CAST. Larger fishes—specimens 10 pounds and over—require stronger casts. This is accomplished by backing the first layer of plastic in the mold with fiberglass cloth or fiberglass matting (Fig. 67) and additional plastic.

When the first plastic layer of the cast has set hard, a glossy surface will appear. Dull it with sandpaper, so the next layer of plastic will adher better. Cut glass cloth with tin snips so as to line the cast inside the mold snugly. The glass cloth is fitted easier if it is cut in sections. Remove the woven glass and spread the plastic reinforced with asbestos over the inside of the cast. Then again place the cloth in position in the cast and spread more of the same mixture over it. Apply some pressure to the spatula so that the plastic will be forced through the weave and thus bind with the plastic underneath. The initial coat of plastic has to be completed in one operation, but the application of woven glass and plastic is accomplished more easily and better if it is done in sections.

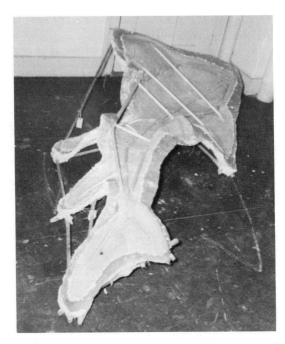

Figure 69. The cast of a shovelnose ray in the mold. A large fish such as this should be strengthened with conduit pipe while the cast is in the mold.

Big-game fishes such as marlin and tuna may be reinforced with two layers of glass cloth and plastic, and further strengthened with pieces of thin-wall conduit (Figs. 67 and 70) or any similar type of pipe. I use conduit because it is light in weight, not expensive, easy to cut and bend, and strong for the purpose. Cut the conduit with a hacksaw and bend it into shape in a vise. The pipe should fit as closely as possible into the contours of the cast. When all the required pieces are placed in position, bind them permanently to the cast with pieces of woven glass and plastic. The conduit will not only reinforce the hollow cast but will supply an attachment for hanging the mount on the wall.

When the plastic material has set, chip away any bits of plastic that may extend beyond the edges of the fish impression of the mold. Now place the halves together and see if they fit snugly. If they do not, it will be necessary to file or chip away the small areas of plastic from the edges of the cast that prevent complete contact of the halves of the mold. The chipped away areas in the back half of the mold, which accommodate the cast fins of the fish, may need additional chipping if there are any irregularities that hinder a good fit of the two sides of the mold (Figs. 41 and 42).

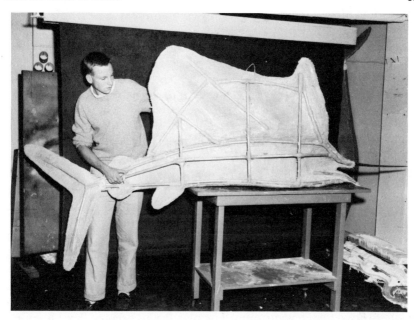

Figure 70. The back side of a large Pacific sailfish showing method of reinforcement with conduit pipe.

SECURING THE HALVES.   Wire the ends of the mold so that they cannot be moved out of position. With a narrow spatula spread the plastic mixture (reinforced with asbestos) along the seams inside the cast where the two halves meet. One application is sufficient to bind the two sections of cast together strongly. In a fish longer than about 30 inches, however, it is a good idea to place narrow strips of woven glass cloth over the seams after the second application of plastic and then spread more plastic over the glass cloth (Fig. 61).

Before putting the halves together, I like to attach a piece of thin-wall conduit along the upper edge of the back side of the cast, although it is not absolutely necessary (Fig. 60). The conduit, which is secured to the cast with plastic, makes a nice, smooth, strong edge for handling the cast. Also, it makes hanging the fish very easy. (See Chapter 15.)

REMOVING CAST FROM MOLD.   Several hours are required for the cast to set hard. To remove the cast from a two-piece mold, first chip away any plastic which may have flowed over the edge of the back opening of the mold (Fig. 62). Tap a chisel between the halves, here and there, until the mold separates. Usually, a bit of jiggling with the chisel at the tail end of the mold will release the back side of the mold first. The whole fish now remains in the show side of the mold. Tap a chisel into the plaster about ¼ to ½ inch away from the cast at the caudal peduncle (Figs. 64 and 65). Then apply pressure to the chisel as you force it down. If there are no outstanding undercuts in the mold, the cast should be removed without complication. If the cast does not release easily, however, proceed to chip away the edge of the mold where it meets the cast. Use care so that the chisel does not damage the cast. Often the troublesome undercuts will be found in the area of the fish's lower jaw. Return to the caudal peduncle, insert the chisel again, and this time the cast should come away easily.

There is another way of joining the halves and removing the cast from the mold. This method produces a full, round cast with no opening on the back side of the fish. Do not saw an oblong piece of plaster out of the back half of the mold, as shown in Fig. 18. Chip away any plastic that extends beyond the edges of the shelf of the plaster mold. This process can be finished by using a disc sander to smooth out any rough edges. The cast from each half-mold is then removed by carefully working a chisel into the plaster in the area just before the tail of the fish. If the cast is obstinate in coming out, place the mold under the hot water faucet and let the water warm the cast for a few minutes. The plastic will become flexible enough to facilitate its removal from the mold. Now place the two plastic halves

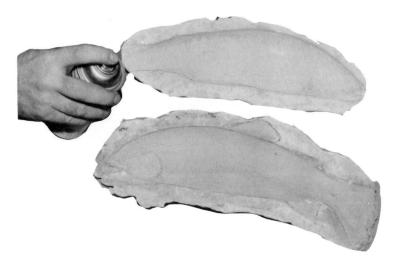

Figure 71. A simpler way of molding a fish at home is to press it into sand and then flowing only one coat of plaster over it. A wide shelf is not necessary. The second half of the mold does not include the tail fin. Household wax or furniture polish, available in spray cans, serves well as a separator before the polyester resin is applied.

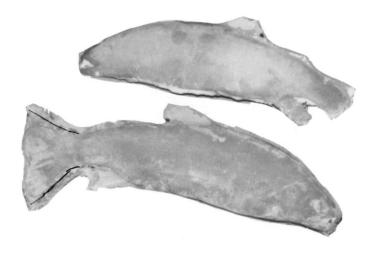

Figure 72. The two halves of the polyester resin cast as they appear when removed from the home-style plaster mold.

Figure 73. Another method of securing the halves together: remove cast from each side of mold (hot water over casts facilitates removal). Hold against each other with stout elastic bands after the resin has been spread along the edges.

together and wrap a couple of rubber bands around them. Run a hacksaw blade through the edges of the halves where they do not fit together perfectly. Remove the rubber bands; lay the two halves on the table and then spread the plastic (a heavy mix with enough filler so it won't run) along the edges of both halves of the cast. Place the halves together and secure in place with rubber bands until the plastic has hardened. If the fish mount is intended to be attached to a panel, secure a block of wood inside the wall side of the cast and glue it there with a fresh mix of plastic. Later the panel can be attached to the cast with screws.

CLEANING AND FINISHING THE CAST.   Usually, in the process of casting, some of the separator wax will be transferred from the mold to the cast. With a cloth dipped in turpentine, rub the affected area until the wax on the cast is removed. Wash the entire cast with a household abrasive cleanser and very hot water. Use a stiff scrub brush. File the edges of the opening in the back side of the cast until smooth.

With a fine-tooth jigsaw (a metal cutting blade is best), cut the excess material from around the mouth, fins, and tail. Mark the outline of the fins with a soft pencil so that they can be followed easier with the saw (Figs. 38 and 39). Do not make the ends of the fin rays too smooth; cut into them a bit in order to produce a more effective, natural appearance.

Use a file to go over the seam where the halves of the cast come together (Fig. 76). It may be necessary to add plastic to the crevices in the seam. A heavy mix of molding plaster and water may be used instead of plastic. Also, use plaster to fill in all the pin holes and to repair any other imperfections in the cast. Another method is to use silver paste and liquid

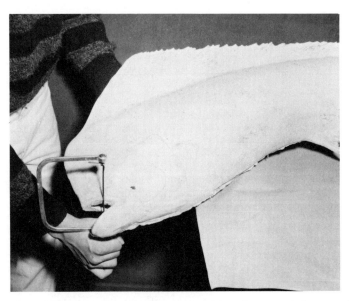

Figure 74.   In open mouth casts, where a mold and a cast of the mouth have been made separately (Figs. 19 and 84), the plastic across the opening of the mouth has to be sawed out. A fine-tooth blade for cutting metal is best.

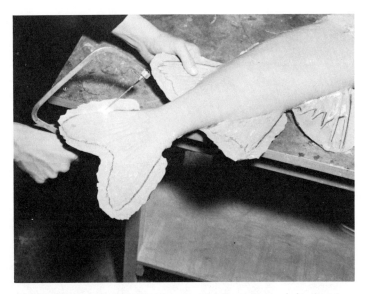

Figure 75. Cut the excess material from around the fins.

Figure 76. The seam of the cast, where the halves have been joined together, is filed and sanded.

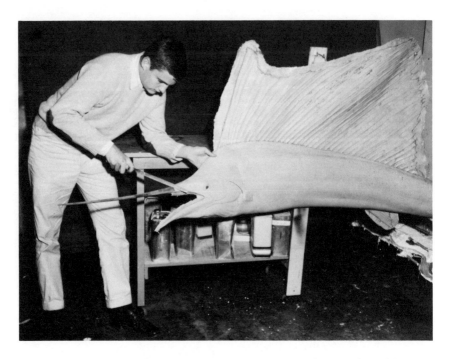

Figure 77. If the original bill of a sailfish or marlin is used, file and sand the area where the bill has been joined to the cast.

Figure 78. The areas which accommodate the bases of the pectoral and ventral fins have been drilled out.

Figure 79. Notice the base of the fin which is shaped to fit the hole. Place resin around the edges of the hole and also around the base of the fin. Then prop the fin in position until the plastic has been hardened.

that is standard for painting radiators. Mix just enough liquid with the paste to facilitate its application. Rub the paste in with your fingers. In this manner all the tiny defects will be filled in. File and sand the areas repaired in plastic. With a pointed tool or small fine file accentuate any necessary lines in the cast, such as those between the jaws, end of the gill cover, and nostrils.

With a drill, cut through the cast in the area where the base of the pectoral and ventral fins will be located (Fig. 78). Also, drill out material from the spot which is to receive the artificial eye. Make the hollow large enough to accommodate the glass eye with room to spare because a substance such as plastic or wax has to be used to hold the eye.

FINS.   If the fins have been preserved and as yet not molded, see "Molding the Fins" in Chapter 2. When the molds of the fins are dried, chisel or dig out the plaster adjacent to the base of the fins on both sides of the mold (Figs. 23 and 25). In this way provision is made for an extension at the base of the cast fin for use when attaching the fins to the body. Shellac and apply separator (same as for body molds) before casting.

To cast the fins (Figs. 80 to 83), use a filler other than asbestos. Spread the substance into both halves of the mold and cover only the impression of the fins. Now place the halves together and apply steady pressure so that the mold halves slowly come together (Fig. 82). Do not press so strongly that no area remains between the halves. On the other hand, do not leave too much space between the halves because the fins will be too thick and

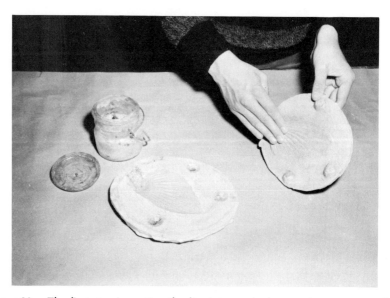

Figure 80. The first step in casting the fins is to apply the wax-kerosene or other type of separator (sprays, etc.).

Figure 81. Apply the resin, reinforced with a filler other than asbestos, to both halves of the mold.

Figure 82. Employ steady pressure so that the mold halves come together slowly.

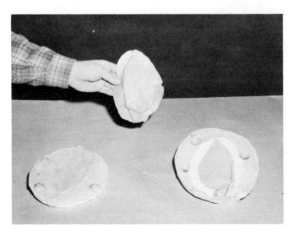

Figure 83. A pectoral fin of a striped bass as it appears when it is removed from the mold.

therefore appear artificial. Do not apply an excessive amount of plastic or you will have to keep wiping the sides of the mold, and this makes a messy job.

When the plastic has set, tap a chisel here and there between the halves of the mold until they separate. If difficulty is encountered in taking apart the mold, it is an indication that the separator was too thin or did not entirely cover the mold surface. Both sides of the mold will never release from the cast fin simultaneously. When one half is removed, the other half will still hold the cast fin. Therefore, it is necessary to insert a chisel gently around the cast in order to pry it away from the mold. Immersion of the mold and cast in hot water or application of heat will soften the cast fin so its removal can be accomplished without breakage.

Clean the casts, wipe off any separator wax with a cloth dipped in turpentine, and wash them well in soap and warm water. Then outline the fins with a pencil and cut them out with a jigsaw. Be sure an extension at the base of the fin remains. Before placing the fins, make sure that you secure a lifelike curvature. This applies to the tail and the fins on the main cast as well as to those that have been cast separately. Let hot water run over them until they become pliable (the pectoral and ventral fins can be held in a small pail of hot water). As you remove them from the hot water, shape them quickly and hold them in position with finger pressure until cool. When cool they again become rigid but remain in their new shape. The fins can be heated and reshaped any number of times. I use cloth-lined

Figure 84. The plastic that had covered the mouth has been cut away. Notice the flowing curves which have been formed into the fins.

Figure 85. The cast of the mouth ready to be inserted—usually through the inside of the head.

rubber gloves so my fingers won't be burned. Under no circumstances attempt to curve the fins when they are not thoroughly heated and pliable, or they will crack.

Now place the pectoral and ventral fins. If they don't fit into their respective holes easily, file away more of the area. Mix a small batch of plastic with heavy consistency; place some around the base of the fins, and insert them. A support is necessary to hold the fins in position until the plastic at their bases has set hard. Some additional application of plastic will be necessary to bring the bases of the fins to their former contours. Use a small file carefully and follow with fine sandpaper to remove rough spots.

MOUTH. If you have made a separate mold of the mouth, prepare it like any other for casting: allow to dry, shellac, and rub on separator. It is best to make the cast in two pieces. Do one side, wait till it hardens, apply the separator to the edges, and then apply the plastic to the other side. After these two pieces have been removed from the mold, they are clinched together with fresh plastic where they meet at the rear of the mouth (Fig. 85). A one-piece cast can be made around the mold, but then it is a chore to dig out the goodly amount of plaster which is in the mouth. The plaster cannot be removed in a single solid form because of the numerous angles and undercuts in the mold.

Trim the cast of the mouth so that it fits accurately into the jaws of the fish, then secure it in place with plastic. It is best to do this from the inside. After this plastic has set hard, fill in the seam where the mouth meets the jaws with additional plastic.

EYE. Paint the glass eye (see Chapter 6). Protect the paint from contact with the plastic, if plastic is used to set the eye in place, by dropping hot wax over the painted side of the eye. If wax is used to set the eye, place the glass eye snugly into the socket while the wax is still soft.

BILLS OR SPEARS. The mold of a sailfish, marlin, or swordfish can be made to include the bill or spear. When the cast is built the bill will also be reproduced in the artifical medium. It is possible, however, to use the original bill in the mount. Prepare the bill as described in Chapter 11. When applying plastic for the cast, place the bill in position and trowel plastic into the base of the bill and the head of the mount or cast. Reinforce the connection with heavy annealed wire, woven glass cloth, and more plastic. Smooth the connection with a file and sandpaper (Fig. 77).

CHAPTER FIVE

Skinning and Skin Mounts

Although it is my opinion that a true, lifelike reproduction of a trophy fish can only be reproduced in synthetic materials, by molding and casting, some anglers prefer to mount the skin. Also, there are times when it is impossible to transport a whole specimen safely home to to a taxidermist. Therefore, to be able to skin a fish properly is a valuable skill, because a salted skin in a plastic container can be carried safely in a suitcase or in the trunk of a vehicle.

SKINNING THE FISH

If the specimen is fresh, remove the slime as described in Chapter 2. If the fish is frozen, thaw it out. Be sure the fins and tail are soft; it they are dried and brittle, damage may occur during the skinning. With a piece of wet cotton dab the fins and tail occasionally to keep them from drying.

A Formalin specimen should be soaked in several changes of fresh water over a day or two and then dunked in a solution of sodium bisulfite and sodium sulfite (see formula 3 in Chapter 15) so that the pungent odor of the Formalin will be eliminated. During the skinning process the fish should be rinsed frequently in fresh water because the skinner's eyes may smart if the fish is not soaked enough. I also advise the use of rubber gloves when skinning a fish which has been preserved in Formalin. There is an advantage, however, to Formlin-preserved specimens because the skin will *never* stretch out of shape during skinning.

The skin, fins, and tail must be kept moist during the process of skinning or else scales will be lost and fins will crack. I prefer to keep the fish on water-soaked cloths while working. Select the show side of the fish and then turn it over; obviously, the cut has to be made on the opposite side. For the initial incision run the knife or scalpel along the midside of the body from the edge of the gill cover to the tail fin (Fig. 86).

Lift the gill cover, insert the scissors into the incision, and point toward the head. Cut through the bony structure that is the piece of anatomy on which the rear edge of the gill cover naturally rests. This step may be done later as indicated in Fig. 91.

Separate the skin from the body along the incision (Fig. 87). Push the knife here and there; use your fingers and thumb as much as possible in the process. Some types of fish skin, however, have to be cut from the body during the entire process of skinning; the skin cannot be pulled away with the fingers. Care should be used not to cut through the skin. If it is damaged, do not panic; it can be repaired in a finished mount. Do not give rough treatment to any fish skin. A mount with many missing scales is not very attractive.

Continue separating the skin from the body until the pectoral fin is reached; snip it at its base. As the skinning proceeds to the other fins, cut them from the body as well (Fig. 89). Exercise caution here because it is easy to insert the tips of the scissors too far and damage the skin. Often, skinning may be facilitated by slicing through and removing a segment of the body (Fig. 88). Carefully skin down to the tail and cut through the body about an inch or two away from the base of the tail. Now, cut through the body close to the head and snip the backbone with a strong pair of scissors. I prefer to use a pair of tin snips. Bend the head down and finish separating it from the body. Continue skinning until the entire body is free. Dispose of the body. Cut the throat skin where it meets the head as indicated in Fig. 92.

Figure 86.   In skinning, the initial incision is made by running a scalpel along the midside of the body from the edge of the gill cover to the tail fin.

Figure 87. Separate the skin from the body along the incision.

Figure 88. Often, skinning may be facilitated by slicing through and removing a segment of the body.

Figure 89. As the skinning proceeds, cut the fins from the body on inside.

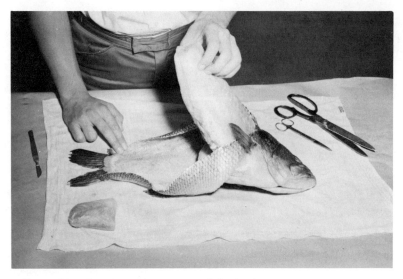

Figure 90. Continue skinning until the body is free up to the head.

Figure 91. Cut through the bony structure, the piece of the anatomy on which the rear edge of the gill cover naturally rests. This step may be done at any process of skinning.

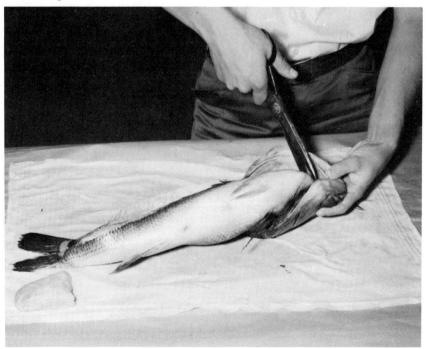

Figure 92. Cut through the throat skin where it is attached to the head.

Figure 93. The skin as it appears with the body removed.

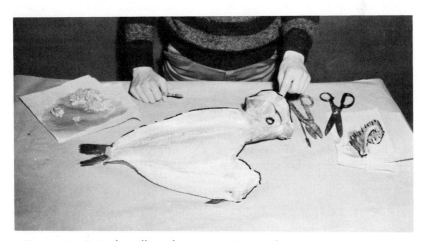

Figure 94. Snip the gills at their extremities and remove them entirely.

Figure 95. Skin the tail to the base of the rays and remove the inch or two that remains. Go over the entire skin and scrape away all bits of flesh.

It is possible, but more difficult, to skin out the flesh in this area while leaving the skin attached to the head.

Return to the head; snip the gills at their extremities and remove them entirely (Fig. 94). Some taxidermists recommend leaving the gills within the head. Why, I don't know. The less flesh, bone, and tissue remaining in the skin the better the mount will be. Remove as much flesh and bone from the head as possible. Gouge out the eyes. Cut into the cheeks from the inside and scrape out all the meat; cut the tongue at its base and remove it. Cut into the skull—of course from the inside—many times with heavy shears or scissors and gouge away as much of the bony structure as possible. If small pieces of the head skin are damaged, they can be repaired in the mounted fish. Return to the base of the fins and cut and scrape away all the flesh clinging to the base of the spines. Then skin the tail to the base of the rays and remove the inch or two of body which remains (Fig. 95). Go over the entire fish and carefully scrape away all bits of flesh from the skin.

Skinning can be interrupted after the body is removed for almost any period of time if the skin is placed in a saturated salt solution. Simply fill a pan with water and add salt until it no longer disappears. Be sure no part of the fish skin remains out of the water.

PRESERVING THE SKIN. If the skin is greasy, wipe it thoroughly and soak it in water containing a strong detergent. There are many good household

soap fluids on the market today; or you can use a strong brown soap. I do
not recommend that the amateur use gasoline or carbon tetrachloride to
remove grease because it is too dangerous. If an adult angler feels he must
use gasoline as a grease remover, he should do it outdoors and a good
distance from home. Under no circumstances should young children use it.

If the fish is well cleaned the only preservative the skin requires (if it has
not been in Formalin) is salt; rub it well into every part of the skin. Roll the
skin up and leave it overnight. A better method is to cover the skin with
salt, place it in a can, and add just enough water to cover the skin. Let it
soak for a day or so. The salt will draw out juices in the skin. Be sure to rinse
out all salt before mounting the skin.

A 10 per cent solution of Formalin is a powerful disinfectant and a
highly efficient preservative. The skin and bits of flesh inside the head can
be preserved better by applying the Formalin with a brush. Do not apply
this liquid, however, until the skin is placed in the mold or ready for
mounting because the Formalin will set the skin in short order in whatever
position it happens to be at the time of application. Be sure to read
Formalin in Chapter 15.

Many taxidermists and teachers of taxidermy advocate painting the
inside of a fish skin with an arsenic paste or fluid preparation; this is
ridiculous. Arsenic is a poison that should not be used by amateurs in fish
mounting, or in any other form of taxidermy for that matter. Bugs cannot
get into a properly mounted fish skin that has been varnished or lacquered,
and that is the purpose of using arsenic—to keep the bugs from eating the
specimen.

I am strongly against using materials such as gasoline and arsenic on
fish skins because there is not necessity for employing such dangerous
items. My first attempt at fish preservation was at the age of five when I
preserved two cunners, partially skinned and housed in a jar of salt and
water. I kept this trophy on a small table by my bed for a couple of years
until the salt ate through the metal cover of the jar. At the age of seven I
caught my first trout—it was a gigantic 14 inches in length. I was beside
myself with concern when I realized that my great trophy would not last
forever in the ice box. With tears in my eyes I cut off the brown trout's tail
and then skinned one side of the fish—minus head and fins. I scraped the
inside of the skin with my penknife. I glued the skin on a neat piece of
cardboard and the tail on another. Many years have passed since that
memorable day, but I still display the skin and tail of that brown trout as
one of the most cherished possessions in my tackle room.

My first whole fish mount was a yellow perch that was skinned and
stuffed with plaster. I filled the eye socket with plaster and painted in a
black pupil. Then I varnished the fish and screwed a backboard to it. I
mounted that perch at the age of nine. The point I am trying to make is that

the trout skin and the perch were not treated with gasoline or arsenic or any type of preservative, and yet they appear to be in the same condition today as they were many years ago.

In the field, when conservation of time is important, it is not necessary to do a thorough job. The body of the fish must be removed from the skin—a job that does not require much time. Also, snip out the gills and eyes. But the head need not be cleaned, and the fine work of removing flesh from the skin and base of fins need not be carried out. However, be sure to do a thorough job of salting.

SKIN MOUNTS

MOUNTED SKINS.   One of the easiest methods of preserving a fish skin for display is to mount the skin of only one complete side. Clean the slime from the fish and remove the skin from the body. Then, with a sharp knife or scissors cut the skin along the median line of the back and belly. Of course, leave the tail and fins on the side of the skin which is to be preserved. Only one of the abdominal or ventral fins will be kept because the skin is cut down the middle of the belly. After cleaning and wiping away as much of the moisture as possible, the skin is brushed with glue (ten parts glue to one part glycerin) and placed on the intended plaque or backboard. Place wax paper over the skin, add layers of newspaper over it, and apply some weight over all. After the fish skin is thoroughly dry, paint it and give the skin and backboard a coat of varnish. An attractive collection of trophies can be produced very easily in this manner. Information on the weight of the fish, and when and where it was caught, can be entered on each plaque to add interest to the collection.

EXCELSIOR BODY.   The most primitive method of fish mounting, which is still practiced, is the placement of the skin over an artificial body or mannequin. The worst type of body for mounting is produced by the use of excelsior and thread over a core of wood. The artificial body must be in the shape of the original but slightly smaller. Then a thin coat of clay, papier-mâché, varnish, or other type of coating is placed over the mannequin so that it becomes smooth and will not absorb moisture. Papier-mâché is stuffed into the head, and the skin is draped around the artificial body. Incidentally, forget about papier-mâché; it is an outmoded material. The excelsior body method of mounting a fish is hopeless; don't use it.

WOOD MANNEQUIN.   This method is an improvement over the excelsior body. Any angler handy with carpenter tools may find it interesting. Outline the fish on paper and then transfer the outline onto a block of wood at least as wide as the body of the fish. A few pieces of wood may have to be glued together. Choose soft wood such as white pine, which is easy to work. Cut out the fish along the outline. If a bandsaw is not available, use any saw and finish the job with a wood rasp. Now, with cutting tools and rasps proceed to produce a wooden body which resembles the original body of the fish as closely as possible—all measurements must be exact. The wooden form should fit into the head of the fish but not tightly—leave some room for casting compound. If the mount is to have an open mouth, cut the wood accordingly. Rough sandpaper the wooden body and then follow with fine sandpaper. The body must be without flaws and absolutely smooth. Apply a couple of coats of shellac to the body, and it is now ready to receive the skin.

Process the skin as described earlier. Brush a thin coat of carpenter's glue and glycerin (see Chapter 15) around the wooden form. Push some casting compound into the bases of the tail and fins, and then place the skin around the form. Tack the skin along the incision on the back side. Now, force some compound into the head and through the mouth and gill opening; build out the cheeks, eye socket, and jaws. If the mount has an open mouth, place more of the compound inside and model it directly as the compound begins to set.

Model the compound into place around the base of the tail and fins by pressing and pushing the material here and there from the outside with thumb and fingers. The fins and tail are soft and pliable but will set in a shrivelled and awkward position unless supported until dried with stiff paper and clips (Fig. 108). Do not pull the fins away from the body. After the fish has dried—the time depends upon weather and amount of heat in a room—clean out the eye socket, add some casting compound or hot wax, and insert the glass eye (see Chapter 6). If the specimen is thoroughly dry, shrinkage will appear about the head—cheeks, lips, jaws, etc. It is not necessary, but if the angler desires a better mount, the head should be reconstructed to its former full contours by brushing on melted wax. If the scales show a tendency to lift, brush a thin coat of glue over them.

Shellac the entire fish. Thin down the shellac with alcohol so that it will flow on easily and not leave brush marks. Screw a piece of wood temporarily onto the back of the fish to support it while painting (see Chapter 6). The best approach is to select a piece of wood 3 or 4 inches wide and about a foot and a half in length. With the fish attached to it, the upright can be placed in a vise and moved up or down to the most comfortable height for painting. Finish the wooden plaque before attaching the fish to it. A screw eye may be inserted into the back of the fish instead for hanging on the wall.

This method of fish mounting is far from the best; however, anyone handy with tools will find it fun, even though styrofoam and other light plastic materials that work easier than wood are available today. With care

Figure 96.   This rainbow, a skin over a wooden body, was mounted by the author in 1938. It has never needed repair and is in surprisingly good condition.

a pleasingly presentable mount can be achieved. Forty-two years ago the first taxidermy job for which I received payment was a 16-inch rainbow trout. I put my heart and soul into a mount that was done by the above method. The mount still looks presentable. I have tried to buy it back from Dr. Joseph DeVita, a veterinarian, for whom I did the job. I would love to have it in my tackle room as a memento. However, he attaches as much sentimental value to it as I do. The rainbow remains displayed proudly in his office and he will not sell. I did manage to photograph it, however, as Fig. 96.

SKIN MOUNTS—HALF MOLD.   One of the easiest ways to mount a fish is to use a one-side mold as a guide or form to fill out the skin with molding plaster or casting compound. A mold for this purpose does not have to be clear in scale definition, nor have a smooth shelf, nor do the fins have to be included in the mold. This method requires less time than any other in molding.

Construct a wooden box big enough to allow 4 or 5 inches of room on all sides of the fish. The sides need not be more than a few inches high (Fig. 97). Place a piece of newspaper inside this receptacle to act as a separator between the plaster and the wood. Pour the plaster directly into the box. Then place the fish gently on the soft plaster and press it in slowly until the midline of the back and belly is reached. The underside of the fins and tail now are in contact with the plaster. Before the plaster has thoroughly set, dig away some of it from around the ventral fins so that they are not buried. When the plaster has set, remove the fish and skin it.

Place the skin in the mold. Check carefully to see that every portion of the skin fits accurately into the mold. If you wish to brush a 10 per cent solution of Formalin on the inside of the skin, head, and body, now is the time to do it.

Fill the downside of the body with plaster or casting compound. If plaster is used, it should be mixed to a heavier consistency than for molding—like whipped cream. Spoon it into the head; press well forward to be sure it fits all parts. Work smartly; the plaster has to be of the proper consistency to push around, but that is only a step away from setting. Place a piece of looped wire into the back of the plaster. Turn the ends so that the wire cannot pull out. This will serve well for hanging the fish on the wall. A piece of skin may have to be cut to accommodate the wire. Obviously, the wire should be shaped and ready before the plaster is mixed. Sew the skin together after the plaster has set in the body.

If the fish is intended to be attached to a wooden plaque, insert a piece of wood into the plaster while it is still soft (Fig. 105). The wood should be waterproofed by dipping it in hot paraffin wax. It can also be made moisture-resistant by lacquering, painting, or some other method. Here again, it is obvious that the wood has to be prepared before attempting to mix the plaster. The plaque is attached to this piece of wood with a couple of screws. Drill holes in the plaque which will allow the screws to be dropped in freely up to their heads. Drill holes of a smaller diameter into the wood in the fish, which will accommodate the screws. If holes are not drilled, the wood may crack; or fins may be damaged due to the craftsman's struggle with the screwdriver. Of course, the plaque should be stained and varnished before attaching the mounted fish to it. During the entire process the fins and tail should be kept moist so that they will not dry and crack.

Casting compound can be substituted for plaster in the same one-sided mold method. Using compound has an advantage because it can be mixed to a puttylike consistency and may be either troweled into the fish or worked with the fingers. Also, there is no urgency to work fast because compound mixed with plaster and water requires much more time to set.

Fill the head and line the body with about a ½-inch layer of compound. Insert the waterproofed wood block. I would recommend a piece of wood that is the shape of the body of the fish only smaller. The head end of the wood should be cut down so that plenty of room remains for compound. Place enough of the compound around the sides of the wood to fill out the skin to its former shape. Tack the skin to the block of wood after the compound has hardened. Care for the fins and finish the fish as described previously.

Whether using plaster or comopund it is advantageous, although not necessary, to preserve the fish in Formalin (10 per cent solution) for four or

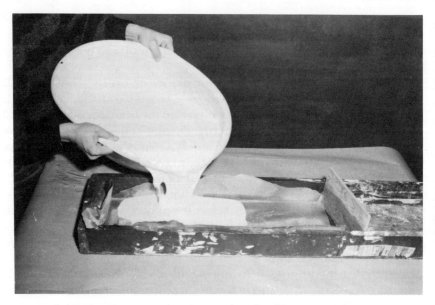

Figure 97. Pour the plaster into a boxlike receptacle.

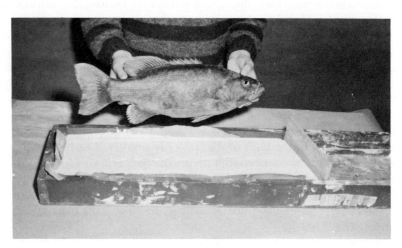

Figure 98. The "show side" of the smallmouth bass will be inserted into the plaster.

Figure 99. Set the fish gently into the plaster so that exactly half of the body has sunk into the plaster.

Figure 100. When the plaster begins to set, dig it out from around the paired ventral fins so that they will be free.

Figure 101. Place the skin in the mold. Check carefully so that every portion of the skin fits accurately.

Figure 102. The skin is now ready to receive the plaster (casting compound mixed with water and plaster can be used instead of plaster).

Figure 103. Pour the plaster into the skin to a thickness of about ½ to ¾ of an inch.

Figure 104. Reinforce with sisal dipped in plaster.

Figure 105. Here you can insert a piece of wood, which has been waterproofed with lacquer or hot wax, directly into the plaster. The wood will serve as a base for attaching screw eyes or hanging wire, or a backboard can be screwed into it. A wire for hanging the mount can be inserted into the plaster instead (while the plaster is still soft).

Figure 106. It is better to chip away a bit of the mold so that the mount will release easily rather than to force the fish out of it.

90

Figure 107. The smallmouth bass as it appears when removed from the half mold.

Figure 108. Cut stiff paper or thin cardboard to the shape of the fins. Secure the two pieces to each fin with paper clips until they dry.

five hours so that the skin becomes rigid before molding the fish. For this method the fish need not be injected with Formalin.

SKIN MOUNTS—FULL MOLD.   For the most lifelike results in skin mounts, I recommend the following method. Preserve the fish in Formalin (see Chapter 1), taking care that it is properly posed. A fish the size of a 16-inch trout or bass will require a few hours or an overnight immersion to harden the skin into shape. When ready for molding, remove the fish from the Formalin and let it soak in fresh water for a few hours. Change the water a couple of times.

Before starting to mold the fish, place a good wad of clay around the pectoral and ventral fins. Disregard the wall side pectoral fin. Shape enough of the clay around the fins so that the ends will protrude through

Figure 109 & 110.   The brook trout (above) and the largemouth bass (below) are excellent examples of exaggerated or distorted anatomical features produced by the taxidermist into unnatural or grotesque effects.

the plaster. In other words, there will be holes in the mold. Wet strips of newspaper will do in a pinch. (Did you know that if newspaper is torn with the grain, long smooth-edged strips are obtained, while against the grain the strips are short and ragged edged?) This procedure will leave large enough holes in the mold to allow a place for the fins when filling the skin with compound.

Make a two-piece mold. Separate the halves, remove the fish, and place it in water so that the skin and fins will not shrivel. After the mold dries, saw out a slab of plaster lengthwise, about 2 inches wide in a mold of a 16-inch fish. Of course, the mold half which has taken the impression of the backside of the fish is the one to cut (Figs. 38 to 40). Dig out the clay placed around the fins before molding. It is best to continue the holes right through the mold if plaster has entirely covered the clay.

Skin the fish, rinsing it in water whenever the Formalin becomes irritating. Cut a piece of skin out of the backside of the fish about the same size and shape as the piece of plaster sawed out of the mold (Fig. 102). Wipe all excess moisture from the skin and place it on a flat surface; fill the head and trowel casting compound onto the inside of the skin to about ½ inch. Pour beach sand or some other dry grainy material into the fish. Place the two flaps of skins back to their original position. Now insert the fish carefully into the show side of the mold; insert the pectoral and ventral fins into their respective holes. Work the other half of the mold into position; be careful not to crease the skin of the fish between the edges of the mold. The skin may required trimming to coincide with the opening in the backside of the mold. Bind a piece of wire around each end of the mold so that the two pieces will stay snug. With the fingers, press and push the sand around gently against the skin. Pour in more sand. Continue to work along until the fish will not hold any more sand.

The next day let the sand run out of the mold by turning it over. Do not, as yet, separate the mold halves. Set it aside to dry in a warm room or outdoors. Gradual drying is best. After a couple of days check the compound; if it has hardened, remove the specimen from the mold and store it in a safe place until thoroughly dry. If the fins or tail need to be shaped, relax them by tying water-soaked cotton around each. Then treat the fins as described earlier in this chapter.

Before painting the specimen it is best to wait until the fish dries—a couple of weeks or more, depending on drying conditions. If the head shrinks noticeably, return it to its former full contours by applying hot beeswax and modeling into shape. A mount of this type looks best without a plaque or backboard. If one is desired, however, fasten a piece of wood inside the fish with cotton and anchor permanently by applying hot wax over the cotton. The backboard can then be screwed to the wood which is inside the fish.

CHAPTER SIX

Painting the Mount

There are numerous ways of painting a trophy so that it will look attractive. The various methods include a wide range of techniques. In other words, there is a method that can be satisfactory for every degree of interest or ability, from a single application of one color for a silhouette effect to the exacting reproduction of the true coloration of live fishes which can be accomplished only by a skilled artist.

PREPARING THE SURFACE.   For painting, the mount first requires a surface which is not porous, whether the trophy is a silhouette on a piece of wood, a skin mount, or a cast. Shellac is satisfactory for this purpose; it is easy to apply and dries quickly. Dilute white shellac 50-50 with commercial alcohol, which can be obtained at any paint shop. Refrain from excessive brushing, or brush streaks will appear. One coat is usually enough for skin mounts or casts produced in plasticlike materials. Wood silhouettes and casts in plaster or casting compound may require more. Plaster usually takes several coats. Brush on one coat, wait until it dries, and then brush on the next—until a sheen or gloss appears indicating that the plaster no longer absorbs the shellac. When the last coat dries, the trophy is ready for painting.

SIMPLE PAINTING.   In medallion-type trophies cast in plaster of Paris, wax, casting compound, or plastics, excellent results can be obtained by simple methods. For example, spray the entire mount with a copper, silver, or gold spray. These days this is a simple procedure. All paint stores carry handy little cans of all sorts of sprays that produce metallic effects. These sprays are inexpensive; many fish can be done with one can. They are easy to work by pressing a button or lever, and their substances dry quickly. The angler may like to experiment with bronze and oil colors to produce a patina effect (the green rust or aerugo that covers ancient bronze sculpture).

94

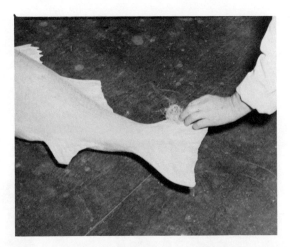

Figure 111. The first step in painting the fish is to prepare the surface. Fill in any pinholes with plaster or a thick puttylike mixture of ordinary radiator silver paste. If plaster is used, go over the fish with sisal to smooth out any irregularities.

Figure 112. Place the mount on a stand of convenient height for painting.

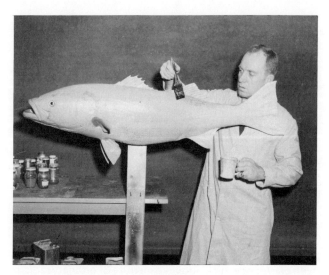

Figure 113. Go over the entire fish with shellac diluted 50-50 with commercial alcohol.

Figure 114. Wait until the shellac is well dried before painting.

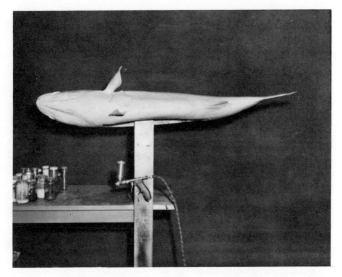

Figure 115. Paint the belly-side of the fish—nearly always a flat white.

Figure 116. Then turn the mount around and paint the dorsal surface—usually bluish-green, brownish-green, or dark blue.

Figure 117. Cover the lateral surface with pearl essence or chrome. Often, a light coat of flat white is applied first, as a base.

Figure 118. Now put in the fine markings with a brush; or if using spray lacquer, employ a small air brush as the author is doing above.

Figure 119. Finally, put the finishing touches on the fins. If spraying the paint, place a paper in back of the fin to protect the body from paint.

Figure 120. In order to bring out the modeling (spines and rays) spray a bit of black or brown across the fin—almost in a parallel position so that the paint hits only the high spots.

Figure 121. The wall side of the fish need not be painted carefully since it won't be seen.

99

Figure 122. The finished striped bass waiting to be varnished or sprayed with clear enamel; two coats should be applied. Be sure the first coat is thoroughly dry before applying the second coat.

Figure 123. A freshly painted king salmon. The specimen weighed 52 pounds when taken in Alaska by the author.

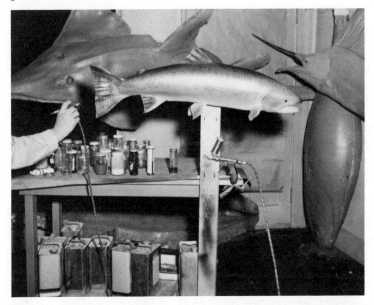

Figure 124. Airbrushing the black spots on the tail of a Deschuttes River Steelhead.

If the angler prefers something closer to the true color of his fish but does not have the talent to paint skillfully, he may delve into a stylized type of painting. For example, a yellow perch has a yellow body, black vertical bars, dark fins on top, and orange-pink ones on the belly side. Oil colors as they come out of the tube (plus a vehicle such as turpentine) can be used without any attempt at mixing pigment and attaining the gradations in coloration of a fine painting. However, the correct number of bars should be reproduced; and if a fish has spots, about the same number should be copied. In other words, a stylized method is a diagrammatic sort of painting which anyone can achieve. And results are surprising; about a half dozen species of fish done in this manner make an eye-catching collection.

PAINTING WITH OILS AND BRUSH. If an attempt is made to approximate the colors of the fish with oil colors and a brush, notes or color transparencies or both should be taken of the fish as soon as possible after it comes out of the water.

Most fishes have a silvery base under the body colors which can be imitated by spraying chrome or silver over the mount before attempting to paint. Pearl essence is also excellent for this purpose. Commercially, it is made mostly from scales of silvery fishes, and it is now available in synthetic form. This pastelike material must be mixed with lacquer and lacquer thinner.

Pigments should not be applied to the mount the same as to a canvas, for oils are much too heavy and the mount would appear artificial. An oil color as it comes out of the tube cannot be used alone; it requires a vehicle to carry it smoothly over the area. A combination of linseed oil and turpentine makes an excellent vehicle. A type of linseed oil named "Stand Oil" is best; it has gone through a heating process which produces a thicker, more viscous oil. It has other desirable properties—pale color, less tendency toward after-yellowing, and a hard, durable finish. It also allows brush marks to flatten and disappear. The Stand Oil should be diluted with an equal amount of rectified (extra refined) pure, clear gum turpentine. Mix the color on a palette or other suitable surface, dip the brush into the vehicle (oil plus turpentine), then onto the oil color, and apply to the mount.

Every finished mount requires a hard, durable surface, such as varnish, as a protective coating. Allow the oil paints to dry thoroughly for a week or so before applying the varnish. Convenient spray cans of enamel or lacquer can be used. Clear varnish, brushed on, is also an excellent covering. Do not apply the first coat of any of these substances too heavily, or some of them may cause the paint on the mount to run. Artists' retouching varnish can be used safely over oils. It is a quick-drying, light-bodied, colorless varnish composed of selected pale resins. These materials can be obtained from any art shop.

PAINTING WITH LACQUER AND AIRBRUSH. Most professionals use lacquers and spray guns (compressed air) for painting fish mounts. An experienced worker can produce excellent results in a short time with this method. The lacquer dries almost instantly upon hitting the mount which, of course, is a great advantage; no dust adheres, and one color can be placed over another immediately to obtain depth and accuracy in color. Anyone having access to compressed air (some machines and tanks are small and portable) should try it.

Proceed in this manner: first, mix the paints. Small instant coffee jars with screw tops serve admirably as receptacles. Pour 2 inches of lacquer thinner into the jar and squeeze 2 or 3 inches of tube oil color into it. Mix well with a brush until the oil color has dissolved and is held in suspension. Add the same amount of clear lacquer as lacquer thinner; stir it. The mixture is now ready for the spray gun. Some brands of lacquer may be heavier than others. If the mixture is too heavy to go through the air gun smoothly, add more thinner. In other words, mix the color, thinner, and lacquer in proportion to suit the situation, although 50-50 lacquer and thinner usually works well.

First, spray the basic color—flat white, silver, or chrome—over the entire surface. Then, turn the mount on the support so that the belly can be sprayed easily (Fig. 115). The great majority of fishes have a flat white belly; therefore, a rather good load of white oil color should be included in the lacquer-thinner mix. On occasion, if results with the airbrush are not white enough, I apply white pigment directly from the tube to the belly of the fish with a brush dipped in lacquer.

Now turn the fish around to a position which will bring the back or dorsal surface toward you (Fig. 116). Be careful not to touch the sprayed surface too soon. If the paint was applied a bit too heavily, it may still be wet. If your fingers have touched the mount in this condition, the paint will adhere to them. If this happens, it will be necessary to remove all paint and start over again.

Most fishes have a blue-green back. Therefore, spray the green on lightly and then go over it with blue; usually emerald green and Prussian blue are the best to use. A light spray of raw umber or raw sienna may be required, and then another touch of green over it. Now, attend to the side of the body with light sprays of the required colors. Do not apply the lacquer colors heavily or the basic silvery sheen will be lost. Up to this point, a medium-sized air gun may be used. For the finer painting required in doing the fins, jaws, cheek and body markings such as spots, bars, or lines, a small airbrush is required. When the paint job is completed, apply a couple of coats of clear enamel. Do not use lacquer for the finish coat because there is danger of the colors running. Lacquer with as little thinner as possible may be used, but still the colors underneath may run or soften because the heavier lacquer has time to affect them.

If your local art shop cannot supply you with a book concerning use of an airbrush or techniques of oil painting try Reel Trophy Inc., P.O. Box 19085, Portland, Oregon, 97219.

PAINTING THE GLASS EYE.   Painted glass eyes can be purchased from most commercial taxidermy supply houses. Unpainted eyes are less expensive, however, and can be painted to match your fish with more accuracy. The blanks or unpainted eyes come with a dark pupil; therefore, only the iris requires painting.

Pour a bit of lacquer (not thinned) into the tin cap of a jar or other receptacle. Dip a small (⅛ inch) brush, which has stiff bristles, into the lacquer, then into a silver or gold powder, and dab the underside of the glass eye. Hold the eye along the edge, bottom side down, and dab the silver or gold (or both) from benath so that you can see the results. Add more silver or gold as necessary. If the iris contained dark specks in life, include these with another small, stiff brush dipped in lacquer and touched to a dark oil pigment such as Vandyke brown. When satisfied that the paint job

Figure 125. Pieces of weather-worn stumps or driftwood, such as the above with a brook trout make excellent bases for shelf or table mounts.

Figure 126. The brook trout in Fig. 125 was attached to the stump by bolt and nut. The head of the bolt was inserted through a drilled hole in the back side of the cast and secured with polyester resin. It is best to perform this operation before the halves are placed together permanently.

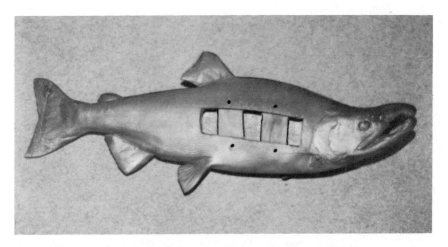

Figure 127. Another method of securing the mount to a panel or hanging it on a wall: two blocks of wood are secured to the back side of the cast after a rectangular piece is cut out of it. The mount then can either be attached with screws through the panel or it may rest on nails in the wall.

Figure 128. The same mount of a sockeye salmon (spawning color and anatomy) resting on nails against the wall.

Figure 129. The above largemouth bass makes a pleasing and beautiful mount because the fish's mouth is not stretched or distorted, and the backboard is rustic and picturesque.

Figure 130. A brown trout mount on a rustic base will look good on any shelf, table, or desk. A screw holds the fish to the base.

looks convincing, pour a few drops of lacquer (not thinned) over the back of the eye. Do not brush the lacquer on as the speckled effect of the iris might be softened. If fresh plastic is used to set the glass eye in the mount, drop hot wax over the lacquer for additional protection. Do this by holding a piece of beeswax over the eye and then touching the wax with a small hot tool. The wax will melt and drop over the eye.

CHAPTER SEVEN
Freeze-Dried and Embalmed Fish

Technicians have been trying for many years to develop a quicker method of preserving fishes for display as trophies of angling success and as specimens for museum exhibition. All such attempts have failed. The failure is not in the lack of preservation, but in the quality of a product that does not resemble a live fish. The specimens appear shriveled and shrunken. Three basic methods have been investigated by many amateur and professional technologists: Formalin and water mixture; embalming by injection; and freeze-drying.

Formalin, a colorless liquid with a nose-curdling odor and vapors that are highly irritating to mucous membranes, is a preservative and a disinfectant that is an excellent medium for preserving specimens in an aquatic state in jars. When removed from the solution after several days, the moisture evaporates from the fish and leaves it looking, as you might expect, like a dried fish. Interesting displays, however, can be made from fish heads—especially those with spectacular dentition like pike, pickerel, barracuda, bluefish, and king mackerel. The eyes of the fish can be removed and glass eyes inserted to make the head more attractive (see Chapter 11).

A few years ago, a commercial company advertised a "complete kit" for embalming, including syringe, a secret solution, and instructions for an injection that would preserve the fish in its original state. The advertising literature displayed a photo of one of the fishes cut in two to demonstrate that the flesh had turned hard "like marble." Any inventor who could come up with such a simple process to preserve a fish indefinitely in a lifelike form would be a millionaire overnight. Unfortunately, no millionaires resulted from that project.

The freeze-dried system for preserving an animal is the same, whether it be fish, reptile, or mammal. Moisture is drawn out of the frozen specimen until it is dry enough to last indefinitely at normal temperatures, with no odor or decomposition. Small mammals, such as mice, squirrels, and rabbits, as well as some birds, freeze-dry best because fur and feathers hide the wrinkled skin underneath. Snakes reflect the shrinkage that has taken place and appear wizened. Freeze-dried fishes, in my estimation, are a total failure; shrinkage, wrinkling, and anatomical distortion are obvious.

Specimens intended for freeze-drying should be delivered to the technician as quickly as possible, fresh or frozen. The technician arranges the specimen in the desired position, freezes it, and then places it as is in a freeze-dry chamber which is held at -20°F throughout the process. Once a week the specimen's weight is recorded. Weight is reduced as moisture is drawn out and is stabilized upon completion of the process. The eyes will not freeze-dry, therefore they have to be replaced with glass eyes. Birds and mammals are preened to look natural and must be sprayed with insecticide because the dried flesh and viscera remain edible and invite boring insects. Paint, lacquer, or enamel sprayed over the fish is a deterrent to insects.

Several taxidermists in the United States practice freeze-drying of trophies. Perhaps the best source of information concerning freeze-drying may be obtained from Ward's Natural Science Establishment, P.O. Box 1712, Rochester, New York, 14603. Other sources of information may be secured from *Modern Taxidermist* magazine and other sources listed in Chapter 15.

CHAPTER EIGHT
Outlines and Silhouettes

The fun of angling includes the discussion and display of catches. Anglers love to establish permanent records of their prowess with rod and reel. For the angler who cannot spare the time or who perhaps does not possess the manual dexterity to produce a more complete type of trophy, I strongly suggest one of the methods treated in this chapter.

All of these processes, even the most simple ones, produce satisfying results. I know. I have about twenty mounted specimens in my home, some of which are exceptional fish; yet my guests are most interested in a few art-board silhouettes of local fish adorning the walls of my tackle room. I suppose this is so because it stimulates the desire, present in the breast of every angler, to display catches to friends—and here are easy, attractive ways of doing it.

PEN AND INK OUTLINES. An outline record of a trophy fish may be a simple tracing in pencil on a piece of brown wrapping paper, which the angler may unroll or unfold for show. With a bit more effort, however, a permanent, decorative piece can be produced instead.

First, wipe the excess slime off the fish. Place the specimen on a fairly heavy grade of brown paper or any other strong paper and carefully trace the outline of the fish using a pencil with soft lead (Fig. 132). When making a tracing around a fish, it is difficult to obtain a clean, smooth, detailed outline, and no matter how well the fish is wiped some slime will always remain on the paper. Therefore, the outline has to be transferred to another piece of paper in order to remedy the flaws. For this step I suggest a better grade of white paper that lies flat. The original outline can be cut out and used as a stencil for tracing the fish onto the white paper; carbon paper can also be used. If no carbon is handy, one can accomplish similar results by covering the approximate area of the outline on the back side of the brown paper with a pencil with a soft grade of lead. Place the brown-paper

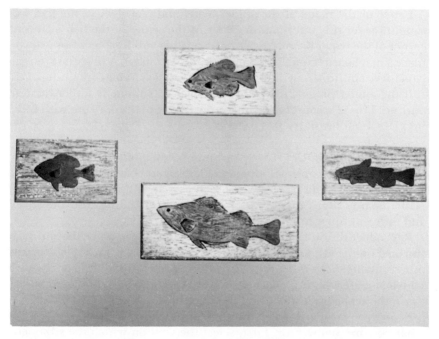

Figure 131.   Silhouettes cut out of wood and glued to a rustic backboard are always attractive.

outline over the white paper to trace the drawing. Apply a bit of pressure with the pencil, and the outline will be transferred to the white paper.

The drawing on the white paper is still rough, so proceed to smooth out irregular lines, erase here, add there, and in general finish the outline. Perhaps you can improve the outline of your trophy by using, as reference, a photo of your fish or an illustration in a good fishing book.

With a pair of sharp scissors, carefully cut out the outline of the fish. Center it on the final art board (art shops have a variety of stiff paper board you can choose from), and tack it lightly with masking tape in two or three places so that the cutout of the fish will not move. Trace it *lightly*. Remove the outline and touch up the sketch where necessary *lightly*. When you are satisfied that the drawing is final, go over it with pen and ink. The ink to use for this purpose is black drawing ink known as India ink. The width of the line is a matter of preference. Line drawings in outline form look better when they are done in heavier lines. All art shops have a wide variety of pens for this purpose. It is not necessary to use the same line width throughout the entire drawing. You may like to put in finer lines for the fin spines and rays or the gill opening.

Letter in the name of the angler, date, and place where the fish was caught. Enter this information either in the center of the fish or in one corner of the paper board. Your trophy outline will look handsome if you place a mat board frame, 2 or 3 inches wide, around it. A first-class job can be achieved by finishing the project with a wooden frame containing glass.

If the angler prefers, the fish can be a solid silhouette rather than an outline. This is accomplished by simply filling in the drawing with India ink. Use a soft brush for this purpose.

ART BOARD SILHOUETTES.   Any angler with a bit of artistic sense can enjoy producing trophy silhouettes of fish in art board. Art shops carry a variety of interesting paper boards such as mat, illustration, bristol, and poster boards. Many different shades of color, including gold and silver, and different finishes are available.

Reproduce the outline of the fish as described above. When the outline is finished on the art board, cut it out with a single-edge razor blade or any other suitable sharp instrument. In order to protect the table or desk top on which you are working, place a piece of glass, wood, or cardboard underneath the art board before using the razor blade.

Before you browse through the materials in the art shop, have an idea of what you are looking for. First, select the wall on which the silhouette mount is to be displayed. Is it pine paneled? If so, is the paneling stained, or is it a natural finish? Is the wall blue—light blue or dark blue?

Figure 132.   Place the specimen on a fairly heavy grade of wrapping paper, or any other strong paper, and carefully trace the outline onto it using a pencil with soft lead.

Figure 133. The completed first draft outline of the largemouth bass.

Figure 134. The paper fish has been cut out and placed on black cardboard. Next, a tracing is made onto the cardboard.

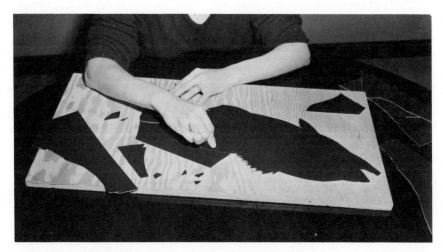

Figure 135. A razor blade is used to cut out the silhouette. If the edge of the black cardboard is gray or white, brush black India ink over it.

Figure 136. Another trophy largemouth bass—black on white with a gold frame.

COLOR COMBINATIONS.   Part of the fun in preparing your trophy silhouette is selecting the colors so they will not clash with the color of the walls and the room decor. If the colors are not right, your silhouette mount will look terrible. But if they are correct your trophy will not only look great, but it will also be an important contribution to the color scheme of the room. If you are a child get your parents in on the project. If you are married, consult your spouse for ideas on color combinations. You will be amazed how much easier it is to get your trophy on the wall if you ask advice on colors!

Some colors go together nicely; others do not. Anglers who have had no experience in art may find the color circle or wheel (Fig. 137) useful for choosing color combinations for fish silhouettes. The color circle is generally accepted as the basic guide in presenting one color with another.

I believe it would not be amiss to discuss color a bit more. Invariably when considering color, the word "spectrum" pops up. The spectrum is a

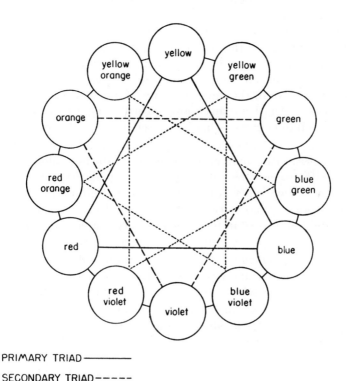

PRIMARY TRIAD ————

SECONDARY TRIAD — — — — —

HUES TRIAD ·······················

Figure 137.   Color wheel. See color combinations in Chapter 8.

continuously varying band of color—red, orange, yellow, green, blue, indigo, and violet. In other words, the spectrum contains, in blended sequence, all colors visible to the eye. In nature, the spectrum is a rainbow.

All the colors in the spectrum are made from three colors: *red, yellow,* and *blue.* Therefore, these are known as the *primary* colors. Any two of the primaries combined produce a *secondary:* red + yellow = *orange;* blue + yellow = *green;* red + blue = *violet.*

The mixing of adjoining colors on the color circle can be carried to more than five hundred varieties.

Basically, there are four types of color combinations or color schemes— complementary, analogous, triad, and monochromatic. These combinations or schemes consist of colors that go well together when used in decorating, and they are equally applicable to art-board fish silhouette trophies.

1. *Complementary Color Scheme.* This setup is called complementary because one color is complemented by a combination of two colors which are equidistant from it on the color wheel. For example, take red; mix the two colors equidistant from it on the wheel (yellow and blue) and you will find its complement to be green. More pleasing effects are usually obtained, however, if the two colors are not of the same intensity. If, for instance, you choose a brilliant red, rather than choosing a brilliant green to accompany it, select a lighter green—that is, a green mixed with white.

2. *Analogous Color Scheme.* Any three colors adjacent to each other on the wheel are analogous; for example, the two colors analogous to yellow would be yellow-green and green (they both contain yellow). Two other colors analogous to yellow are orange and yellow-orange (both also contain yellow). Here, too, all three colors should not be used in the same intensity—rather, use one brilliant and two light or one light and the other grayed.

3. *Triad Color Scheme.* Three colors equidistant on the wheel, such as orange, green, and violet form a triad (again no three of the same intensity). This scheme offers variation without clashing of colors.

4. *Monochromatic Color Scheme.* One color with two or more values of the same color produces a monochromatic color scheme. For example, a light green silhouette on a dark green background.

As I said previously, the color scheme of your room should be the basic criterion for choice of color in your fish silhouette. If you have green walls, your fish may look well cut from an illustration board on the red or maroon side (complementary colors). The background board could be a green lighter or darker than the wall.

If you want a more subtle effect in your room with the green walls, your fish could be a blue-green silhouette or a yellow-green background board (analogous colors).

On a blue walls you might choose a maroon fish on a pale yellow background (colors in triad). If you were looking for a still softer effect on the blue wall, you could choose a light blue silhouette (lighter than the walls) and a very light blue background (monochromatic colors).

Use the colors in the wheel and my suggestions merely as a guide. The final choice should be made mainly by considering the color of the walls, rugs, and all other accessories in the room. Wise choice of a wooden frame may also improve the composition of your silhouette mount. Try different combinations by placing pieces of colored paper against the wall. You will find it fun.

The main wall in my basement tackle room is made of cinderblocks that I have painted light green. Another wall is paneled with stained driftwood. On the green wall I have a series of three fish trophy silhouettes—brown, rainbow, and brook trout. The fish are cut from light maroon illustration board on a white background of poster board, and each is encompassed in a 3-inch frame of dark green mat board. The driftwood wall has a single silhouette—a largemouth bass which is done in gold on a black background with a white frame of mat board. All of them are set in dark wooden frames that have a natural rubbed finish. Each fish has the weight, dimensions, place where caught, and date lettered in black India ink in the right-hand corner. Without fail, every one of my fishing friends and every new member of the Yale Fishing Club who sees my fish-mount silhouettes for the first time exclaims, "This is wonderful; I'm going to start a collection too!"

OUTLINES BURNED IN WOOD.   Fish trophies produced in wood go well in a casual or rustic type of room. A series of fish outlines burnt in wooden plaques add interest to any informal room whether it is a den at home, a child's bedroom, or the main room of a fishing camp. The fish outlined may be of several different species, or the display may consist of a single kind.

You and your family may fish in an area that has several species of fish (for example: bluegill, sunfish, catfish, yellow perch, bass, and pickerel; or along the shore: tautog, cunner, flatfish, bluefish, and striped bass). Have a family competition. Father could be weigh-master and recorder; of course the rest of the family should witness the weighing-in of any fish he catches! A temporary outline of each fish entered is made. As a heavier fish comes in, another outline is traced; and the previous record discarded. At the end of each season, the biggest fish of each species is permanently recorded with its outline burnt in a plaque. The angler's name, date, and place where the

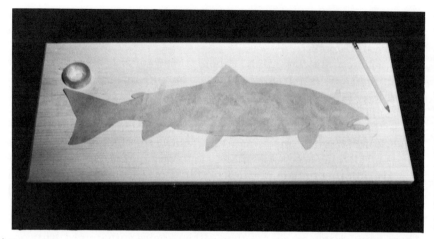

Figure 138. For a burnt-in outline, make a paper cutout as previously described. Then tape the outline of the fish to a piece of whitewood or white pine, and trace around it.

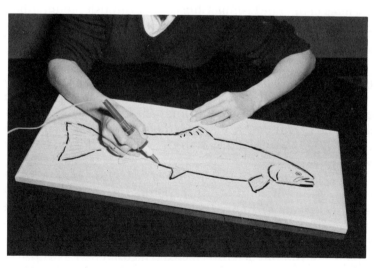

Figure 139. Burn the outline into the wood with an electric "woodburning pen."

118

fish was caught should also be burnt in. It could be great fun to have the final party of the season reserved for the wall hanging of the outline trophies.

George Albrecht and I stayed at a fishing camp, on the banks of the Miramichi River in New Brunswick, Canada, where we took great interest in the burnt-in outlines of Atlantic salmon that lined the walls. Every salmon over 15 pounds taken by anglers who stayed at this camp was burnt directly into the wood of the wall. Each outline was accompanied by the name of the angler and the fly that took the fish. This collection was unusual because the silhouettes dated back many years.

If you intend to make a burnt outline trophy on a plaque, choose a good grade of wood without knots. Clear white pine is fine for this purpose. Outline the fish as described earlier. Be sure to make the initial outlines on paper and then transfer them onto the wood. Otherwise, the wood will absorb some of the slime of the fish and be discolored.

My friend Larry Sheerin of San Antonio, Texas, and I visited Enrique Guerra at his ranch in Mexico. Larry and I watched fascinated as Enrique burnt designs into the walls of his dining room. He had a low fire going in the fireplace, where he heated large branding irons until red hot and then pressed them, sizzling, into the wall. I would not, however, advise anyone to try this method on fish silhouettes. An electrical tool is made specifically for this type of work; it is easy to handle, heats quickly, and is inexpensive. The set includes a main heating unit with a cord attached to it and about

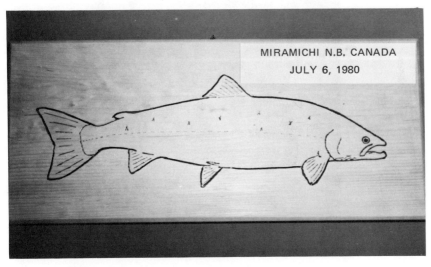

MIRAMICHI N.B. CANADA
JULY 6, 1980

Figure 140.   The finished outline of a grilse (salmon).

six interchangeable pens of different shapes. Commercially, an outfit of this type is known as a "wood-burning pen" or an "electrical pencil set." All art supply stores and hobby shops carry them. If you own a small soldering iron it may be used instead, but it is a bit awkward to employ because the handle of a soldering iron is high, making it hard to manage.

The thickness of the line is a matter of taste. Practice on a piece of scrap wood with the different points before attempting the fish outline. It is beter to go over the entire fish lightly several times, rather than attempting to burn the line deeply into the wood at the first burning. Of course, always apply the stain or varnish to the plaque when all the burning is finished. A fish trophy of this type does not look well with a glossy finish, and the wood looks best natural. Brush on a thin coat of shellac (thinned 50-50 with alcohol). When that is dry apply a coat or two of rubbed-effect varnish (satin finish), available at any paint store.

WOOD SILHOUETTES.   Another easy but satisfying way of making a fish trophy collection is to cut the silhouettes out of wood. Here, again, is a method that can satisfy a wide range of individual abilities.

Fish silhouettes in wood can be an excellent project for boys who like to fish and who also like to handle tools. The outline should be produced on the wood as described previously. If the child is just learning to handle

Figure 141.   First outline the yellow perch on a piece of ¼-inch plywood.

Figure 142. The outline can be touched up after observing the fin structure.

Figure 143. The outlined fish is cut out of the piece of plywood.

121

Figure 144. The edges of the wooden perch are filed and sanded. A wooden pectoral fin is glued on.

Figure 145. Flat black paint is applied.

Figure 146.   The finished trophy.

tools, I would suggest ¼-inch plywood for the fish silhouette. The wood can be clamped to a table to make sawing easier, or it can be held by hand as shown in Fig. 143. The edges of the fish should be sanded, and the spot for the eye can be drilled. Stain the silhouette and glue it to a ½-inch pine plaque with beveled edges.

Any angler who is handy with tools can have fun making a series of wooden silhouette trophies that require more care. For example, the silhouette can be cut from ¾- to 1-inch stock. A power jigsaw or bandsaw should be used. The edges of the wooden fish can be beveled with a rasp, or the edges can be rasped until a "half round" effect is achieved. The eye should be hollowed out with a drill. The lines denoting the gill opening, jaws, fin rays, and so forth can be carved in with appropriate tools. Another way is to cut out just the body and tail of the fish, and then insert fins sawed from material such as ¼-inch plywood. In this case, slits in the wooden body will have to be gouged out—use a drill and then a chisel. Also, leave a base on the fins which can be inserted into the recesses and held with glue. A glass eye glued in will give the trophy added sparkle. This type of trophy looks good stained dark if placed on a light colored wall, and a natural finish is best if it is situated on a dark wall. I prefer such a silhouette without a backboard or plaque. Letter the pertinent information directly onto the body of the wooden fish, black lettering on a natural wood fish or white lettering on a fish stained dark. A thin coat of shellac (thinned 50-50 with alcohol) should be applied over the stain before painting on the lettering. Complete the trophy with a coat of flat-finish varnish.

CHAPTER NINE

Inked Prints

I first became aware of the attractiveness of inked fish prints more than a dozen years ago when a group of college students from Japan presented me with several outstanding prints during a reception we had for them at my home. The students were en route to Canada where they were to represent Japan in the Annual Game Fish Seminar and Fishing Match that I was directing in Nova Scotia. The team captain told me that the ancient art of printing fish, or *gyotaku* as it is known in Japan, originated in that country many hundreds of years ago.

The prints that the Japanese fishing team brought with them interested me immediately because I realized that these inked replicas could be treated as pieces of art or as aesthetically pleasing records of trophy fish. For the next year's seminar, I asked the Japanese team to bring the materials required to make the fish prints. They gave a demonstration to the other participants—eleven college teams from Canada and the United States—on making the prints one day after we returned from fishing in the famous Nova Scotian waters.

As the Japanese students worked on the prints of local fishes, caught the previous day, I was surprised at how easily the job was done. The print is simply a negative copy produced by inking the surface of the fish and transferring the image to various kinds of paper, including rice paper, construction paper, and colored paper, or plain white cloth, such as pieces of bed sheets.

HOW TO MAKE THE PRINTS.   Remove the protective slime from the side of the fish to be printed. This can be done by rubbing over it a sponge that has been dipped in a solution of one part baking soda and three parts water. Vinegar and water or alum and water can also be used for this purpose. Dry the specimen well with paper towels. Best results are obtained from a thoroughly dry fish.

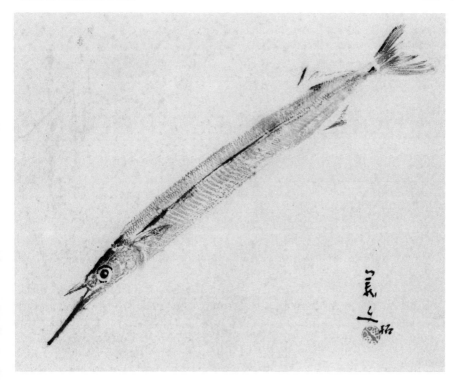

Figure 147.   Inked print.

Place the fish on a flat surface facing in the opposite direction you desire the resulting print to be. Now, with a soft brush, smear the entire side of the fish, including fins and tail, with black ink or acrylic paint (obtainable from any art store or hobby shop). Place the paper or cloth over the fish and pat it carefully with your fingers or a stiff brush. Some types of paper have to be moistened slightly before applying over the fish. (Trials and experimentation will be necessary before a good print is obtained.) Remove the paper or cloth with care, and especially avoid dragging it. When the ink has dried on the print, you can touch up details where necessary by using a small art brush or black felt-tip pen. As you gain experience, you may try different colored inks or acrylic paints. And, if you desire a really professional-looking print, stretch the cloth over a wooden frame and tack it with a staple gun in the same manner as an artist attaches canvas to a frame.

CHAPTER TEN

Photographs as Trophies

Any angler who carries a camera during fishing trips can build a fine collection of fish pictures. Notice I did not say fishing pictures. I have viewed thousands of photographs taken by all types of anglers whose results ranged from the ridiculous to the professional. Almost without exception the photos are either beautiful scenes of the outdoors with the angler as the secondary point of interest, or else the proud angler is standing stiffly, holding the fish in one hand and the rod awkwardly in the other. Most anglers, when posing for a photo, stand against brick buildings, clapboard, fences, and other uncomplimentary backgrounds with dominating horizontal lines. However, with a bit of coaching—and some common sense—any angler can produce excellent photo trophies.

COMPOSITION AND HINTS.   All fishermen love to be photographed with their catches. I'm included. I am not ashamed to say that I have a great many photos of myself with fishes of all kinds. However, I attempt to set up the composition so that the photo will have as little appearance of being posed as possible. For example, if you catch a big trout, don't pose stiffly. Try something like this: sit on a rock at the edge of the stream, put the open creel beside you, and hold the fish in your hands as though you are admiring it. Make it appear as if this is a few minutes' break in the fishing. And don't look at the camera! Think of the composition. Is there another boulder to balance the other side of the photo? Move over a few feet; perhaps a branch of a tree overhead will add interest. A few extra minutes required for a good shot will pay great dividends in pleasing results. If you want the fish to be the point of interest—and it should be in a trophy photo—have the camera close to the angler and the fish. A profile shot of the angler, including his head and chest, as he looks down on the prize is an excellent way to portray both.

However, for a good series of fish trophy photos which will add dignity to any room, I strongly recommend elimination of the angler from the

126

Figure 148. A 12-pound rainbow (all fish in this series were also caught by the author). This photo could have been improved by lowering the fish on the platform to eliminate the ground above it. The tape has been added to prove that the rainbow was 30 inches long.

Figure 149. This photo of a 42-pound bass is given character by posing the fish on a rock.

Figure 150. Montana cutthroats are placed over a creel on the shores of a pebbly stream. An object such as a camera can be positioned strategically to improve the composition and indicate the size of the trout.

Figure 151. A brown trout taken in Encampment Wyoming was posed on the rail of a broken cattle fence. Notice how the wide landing net balances the long, narrow lines of the fence rail and rod.

Figure 152. Here again the creel supplies the bulk necessary to balance the long lines of the Canadian brook trout's body and the landing net.

Figure 153. Good trophy photos need not include exotic game fishes. A big panfish, such as this jumbo yellow perch, can be as effective.

Figure 154. The above trophy-size Labrador brook trout make a pleasing photo by simply placing them informally over a lichen covered rock. Note that the heads are propped up by the rod.

Figure 155. In this photo the background is too busy and distracting. A shot of this lake trout placed on the boat seat would have produced a better photo.

Figure 156. This sheefish was simply placed over a minnow seine and photographed by the author on the banks of the Kobuk River in Alaska.

Figure 157. A limit catch of Arctic grayling crossed against the long parallel lines of a plank makes a pleasing trophy photo that records the occasion.

Figure 158. When fish are photographed with the angler in the scene, the fish should be the dominant or focal point of interest such as the Chinook salmon above which draws the viewer's eye.

Figure 159. A little imagination goes a long way in producing attractive fish photos. These lake trout were posed under water with the trophy-size specimen on top.

picture. Black-and-white photographs lend themselves better to a line or grouped series of fish photos. Colored prints are best for a single picture in one given area of wall space.

Do not place your fish just anywhere on the ground for a shot. If you want to indicate the size of the fish, place your catch so there is a natural object to compare the fish with. Don't place a package of cigarettes or a tape measure alongside the fish. Instead, arrange the fish on a log or over a creel. Lay the rod beside it, or perhaps place your hat, a fly box, or a plug alongside. An interesting shot consists of laying the fish across a landing net; another example—set the fish in a spot along the shore so that a portion of its body lies in the water. Sometimes the fish looks best without accessories, propped on an interesting piece of pebbly shore or sandy beach. Do not take the shot at an unnecessary distance from the fish; fill a good portion of the camera finder with the subject. There are countless arrangements which will prove interesting and artistic. Take a few minutes to look around; give it some thought.

Volumes have been written on cameras, their manipulation, and the actual techniques of photography, so I won't advise the angler on that score. All photography shops stock manuals on photography. Because I have been photographing fish in the field for many years, however, I might add that there are a few simple things that the angler-photographer should keep in mind in order to produce the best kind of trophy photos.

1. Get close to the fish.
2. Look for an interesting composition or arrangement of the subject.
3. Move your camera angle until you find a spot where the least reflection is bouncing back from the body of the glossy fish.
4. Try three or four different exposures of the same shot.

I have found that a series of black-and-white photos look best if they are all mounted identically—usually with a rather wide mat board and a narrow black wooden frame. My brother, Fritz, has a series of six fresh-water fish done in this manner in his study. The photos are placed in a single line about 16 inches above the wainscoting. I must say they look great. Figures 148 to 159 may suggest composition possibilities to anglers.

CHAPTER ELEVEN
Special Trophies

Properly preserved and displayed, various original parts of fish make fascinating trophies. There is something about a head of a fish preserved dry or in Formalin that draws immediate attention. A collection of tails, whether dried or cast, makes an unusual display. Head mounts, of course, always have been popular. And bills or spears of big game fishes have been collected by fishermen since time immemorial. One of my hobbies is collecting the bills of sailfish and making letter-openers of them.

FISH HEADS PRESERVED. A series of heads, preserved dry, makes an interesting collection. The heads can be mounted on plaques for wall decoration, or they can be displayed on shelves. Heads of fishes such as pike, pickerel, barracuda, and bluefish are especially impressive because of their imposing teeth.

Cut the head from the body close behind the edge of the gill cover, taking care not to disengage the tongue. I prefer to remove the gills, although they may be left in the head. Clean out the inside of the skull, and cut away loose flesh and bone. It is not necessary to cut away all of the skull as in a skin mount. It is a good idea, however, to break a hole through here and there to remove the brain and to facilitate the entrance of the preservative solution.

Prop the mouth open with a piece of wood or wire, and place the head in a 10 per cent solution of Formalin. It should remain immersed a week or two to allow thorough saturation by the Formalin. Remove the head and permit it to dry gradually in open air. Do not try to rush the drying by placing the head over a radiator or setting it in the sun. When the head has dried hard, in a matter of a couple of weeks, cover it with two or three coats of enamel or lacquer. Small spray cans of these are obtainable at any paint shop. The eyes can be replaced with glass eyes. However, since a dried head is not meant to look alive, I usually let the eyes dry also. The head can be secured to a stained and varnished base for easier handling. Drill small holes through the lower jaws and attach the head to the base with wire.

138

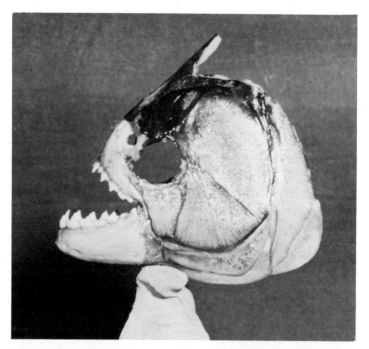

Figure 160. Only the bony structure of this piranha head remains. Notice how the skin has been cut away to display the teeth fully. The head was first preserved in a 10 percent solution of Formalin.

Figure 161. A dried head of a bluefish after it has been preserved in Formalin.

Figure 162. Fish such as pike, pickerel, and barracuda (above) make interesting trophy heads because of their imposing dentition. This barracuda head was also preserved in Formalin.

Figure 163. A king mackerel (kingfish) head also draws attention because of its teeth.

Another way of preserving heads is to remove as much of the flesh as possible, leaving only the bony structure. This can be done with a fresh head or with a Formalin specimen. If a fresh head is used, it is advisable to place the bony structure in Formalin for a few days anyway after it is cleaned. The head can be left in its natural state or sprayed with gold or silver.

FISH TAILS PRESERVED. Tails of all types of fishes are easily preserved. Immersion in a 10 per cent solution of Formalin for a week or so is all that is necessary. Allow the tail to dry gradually in open air; do not place it in the sun or over a radiator. The tail can then be attached to a plaque, or it can be hung on the wall by a concealed wire. Another attractive method (for a big fish) is to tie a ¼-inch rope around the base of the tail, leaving a loop for attachment to a metal wall hanger.

Tails of large fish such as tuna, marlin, and sailfish are especially imposing trophies when dried and painted. The famous Cabo Blanco Fishing Club in Peru, where some of the largest game fishes in the world were taken, has a most impressive driveway in front of the clubhouse—it is lined with posts that have large marlin tails attached to their tops.

A plastic or resin cast of any fish tail, painted in the original colors, is especially effective. It can be attached to a plaque, and the angler's information can be painted on or inscribed in metal by an engraver.

HEAD MOUNTS.   Head mounts of fishes are often preferable to full-body mounts, especially of big game fishes such as swordfish, marlin, and sharks. The medium-sized fishes—large striped bass, bluefish, catfish, musky, pike, and bass—also make attractive head mounts.

The same procedure is followed in making a head mold as in producing a regular two-piece body mold, except, of course, that the plaster need not extend more than half the length of the body. Always include the pectoral fin or fins and a portion of the body beyond the fins. Wherever possible (depending on the type of fish), include a portion of the dorsal fin. It is always preferable to make the mold longer than the intended cast, so that the cast or mount may be cut to fit at the desired angle against the wall. This is easier than attempting to make the mold exact. Often a regular body mold that has not been severely damaged when the cast was removed can be used again for producing a head mount. The cast can be made from polyester resin or from casting compound.

A head mount which faces out from the wall at an angle is more attractive than a mount facing out head-on. However, I have made some unusually interesting large catfish heads that were mounted facing directly away from the wall. After the cast has been cut at the desired angle, attach a wooden backboard along its back edges with flat-headed screws countersunk below the surface of the cast. Hide the screw heads with some of the material of which the cast is made.

BILLS OR SPEARS OF BIG FISHES.   The preserved bills or spears of big fishes—sailfish, marlin, swordfish, and sawfish—make excellent trophies. They are comparable to the mounted antlers loved by deer hunters. See Figs. 164 and 165 for ways of displaying these trophies.

Swordfish.   When an angler catches a swordfish, he never releases it, because the flesh of this fish is always in demand and usually brings high prices. Therefore, the angler nearly always cuts the sword off and retains it as a trophy.

Preservation of the sword is simple; actually it requires only drying. As the sword is mostly bony in structure, it may be sawed off from the head and then exposed to the air to dry. In drying, the sword will lose its original color. Some anglers paint the sword as close to the natural color as possible and then apply several coats of lacquer.

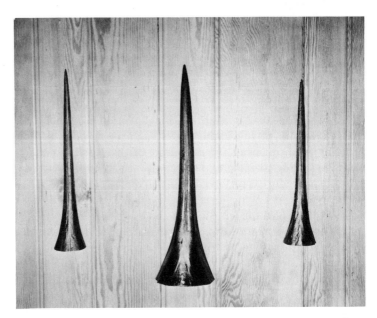

Figure 164. Marlin bills can be situated to advantage on walls.

Figure 165. Marlin and sailfish bills make attractive trophies mounted upright on blocks of wood.

142

If a couple of holes are drilled along one edge and a chain attached, the sword can be hung on a wall. If the angler prefers to have the trophy in an upright position on a shelf or table, a piece of wood should be attached to the base of the sword.

Some anglers prefer to clean or bleach the sword so that it appears whitish. This can be done by immersing the sword in salt water, but this procedure requires much time in soaking. A better method of bleaching is to place the sword in a 1 or 2 per cent solution of potassium hydroxide for about a week in sunshine. The fleshy material will be broken down, leaving the bone whitish. When removed from the solution, the sword should be washed in fresh water and dried.

Sawfish.   The sawfish should not be confused with the swordfish. The swordfish has a pointed, smooth-edged bill. The sawfish's bill has a snub end and about twenty-five sharp, toothlike protuberances along each side of the two lateral edges. Skates and rays are closely related to the sawfish.

A large sawfish is dangerous when being boated. Its toothed bill is a formidable weapon. For this reason, the sawfish's "saw" is a conversation-provoking trophy that all anglers love. It can be given the same preservative treatment as described for the swordfish bill.

Marlin and Sailfish.   The marlin and the sailfish are the most spectacular big-game acrobats in the sea. Any angler fortunate enough to experience fighting one of these beauties certainly would like to have some sort of memento of the occasion at home. It is a comparatively rare angler who has the facilities to accommodate more than one or two mounts, if any, of these big fish on his walls. Therefore, the bills from marlin and sailfish make excellent trophies.

Marlin have been gladly accepted as food by the local people in every big-game area I have fished, except off our American coasts. Anglers who catch sailfish in the vicinity of Florida are asked to release the fish as a conservation measure, unless it is to be used as a trophy. However, smoked sailfish is gaining in popularity. Scientists have also found that the sailfish has a short life span, and its release may not be as important as previously thought. In the future more sailfish may be taken ashore.

The bill of a marlin or a sailfish looks much better if it includes a base rather than just the bill proper. Saw off the bill part way up the head, about an inch or so in front of the eyes. Cut away the roof of the mouth—you may need a hacksaw—and remove all the insides with a knife. A chisel is useful in gouging out the bony material and gristle. Work away until the bony structure of the bill proper is reached and just a shell of the base remains (Fig. 166).

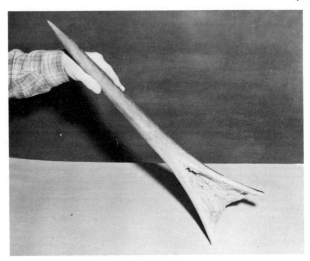

Figure 166. The underside of a black marlin bill. The upper fleshy fore part of the mouth has been removed and only the bony or hard portion remains.

After cleaning out the base, rub the inside with salt. Set the bill aside, well salted, in a pan overnight. This procedure will assist in drawing out the juices. Scrape away again at the base and then wash off the salt. Usually, some grease will remain in the base; therefore, it is a good idea to soak the bill for a few days in a strong detergent or other liquid that has the power to remove the grease but will not harm the bill. Although not always necessary, it is a good idea to place the bill in a 10 per cent solution of Formalin for a few days. Allow the bill to dry thoroughly before mounting.

It is difficult to saw the bill off the head in such a manner that the base is square—that is, so that when placed in an upright position on a table the bill will be perfectly perpendicular to the table top. For this reason, some additional cutting with a hacksaw or a rasp will be necessary later.

The bill makes a better appearance if the base is filled. One method is to fill it with plaster of Paris. Make a heavy mixture of the plaster—like stiff whipped cream—so that it will stay where placed with a trowel. If the bill is to be hung on a wall, insert a looped wire into the plaster while it is still soft. Wait until the plaster is thoroughly dry before applying a couple of coats of shellac to it. Then paint the bill in its natural colors, dark blue on the dorsal surface and light gray or flesh color underneath.

A better way of finishing the base is to cut a piece of ⅛- or ¼-inch wire mesh the shape of the base, and place it in position so that it enclose the bottom and underside. The edges of the wire can be bent in such a way as to hold the mesh firmly in place. Now cut a piece of cheesecloth the same shape. Press casting compound (mixed liberally with plaster and water) into the cheesecloth with a putty knife, and cover the wire mesh with the cheesecloth. When this has set, apply more compound and model the material here and there until it is smooth and finished. Wait until thoroughly dry before shellacking and painting. If the bill is intended to stand upright, trowel some fresh compound onto the bottom of the base and press it down firmly on a greased piece of glass. In this manner the base will be perfectly flat. The grease or Vaseline will prevent it from sticking to the glass. If the bill is to be hung on a wall, insert a looped wire into the base. Polyester resin and glass cloth are superior to plaster or casting compound and cheesecloth in this operation.

SHARK JAWS. Sharks, like snakes, are unusually intriguing to everyone, even though most people may abhor them. These animals have an unexplainable attraction, perhaps because they are considered dangerous and repulsive. Whatever the cause may be, the fact remains that a photo or even just a mention of the word "shark" draws immediate attention. Therefore, the jaws of a shark mounted on an attractive plaque make an excellent trophy. Place a set on your wall and you will soon discover that your guests will make a beeline toward the shark jaws, even though you may have more valuable objects in evidence.

No shark has a true bone in its body. The skeleton is composed of cartilaginous material. The jaws are not hard bone; therefore, care must be exercised when cutting them out of the head. If you cannot work on the jaws immediately, sever the head with a knife and a saw. Dispose of the body over the side of the boat, unless, in the case of a mako shark, you want to cut some steaks from the carcass.

Be sure the shark is dead before you attempt to decapitate him! This is not as silly as it sounds. The shark's jaws that appear in Fig. 168 belonged to a 321-pound mako I caught off the Bay of Islands in New Zealand. We boated that beast shortly after 10 A.M. and lashed him securely atop the stern. His back was lanced severely in a dozen places by our over-enthusiastic mate. The fish was fully exposed to the broiling sun the rest of the day, while we fished. We returned to Otehei Lodge about 7 P.M. and hoisted the mako onto the dock with a rope and pulley. Then I posed myself proudly, with a rod and reel, by the shark which was hanging tail-up, close to the edge of the dock. Just as the photographer was about to take the last shot, the shark suddenly came to life, and with an amazing twist in his body, snapped his jaws—at me, I thought. His sudden action took me by such surprise that I dropped the rod and tried to jump back. There was a 6- by 6-inch railing at my feet so that when I attempted to move, my heels caught the railing. I went overboard. I didn't mind the water so much because I

Figure 167. A 321-pound mako taken by the author in New Zealand.

was ready for a bath anyway, but there were some pretty girls watching me as I posed with my chest stuck out, and it was embarrassing. Since that memorable event, I've had the greatest respect for sharks.

Let us assume that the angler has had no unpleasant experience and still wishes to remove the jaws. A sharp knife is essential. Do not attempt to cut through the hide to get at the jaws. Instead, start cutting from inside the mouth. Keep slicing through the flesh and skin from the teeth downward in the lower jaw. Do not use the knife too ambitiously or the cartilaginous jaw will be cut.

When separation is complete around the outer side of the lower jaw, turn the head around and repeat the process with the upper jaw. With some pulling and cutting of gristle and cartilage, here and there, the jaws will come away from the main body of the head. Do *not* disengage the jaws where they meet at the angle. Now commence to cut along the inside, starting from the angle of the jaw and working forward. Cut and scrape away all bits of meat and gristle that may be adhering to the jaws, and then rub salt on them and let it stay overnight. The salt will draw out the juices

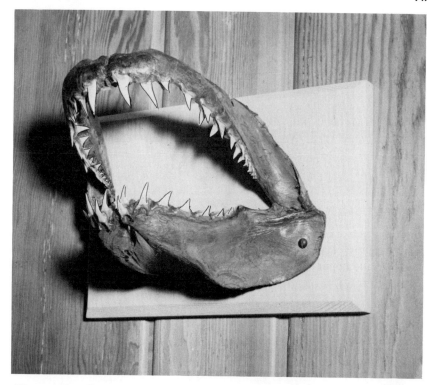

Figure 168.   The jaws of the same shark in the author's tackle room at home.

and the next day the extra matter adhering to the jaws can be scraped away more easily. Rinse the jaws in clean water and lay aside to dry. Prop the jaws apart with pieces of wood while drying, or the jaws will pull together out of position.

When the jaws are thoroughly dry, they can be smoothed a bit with sandpaper to make a better appearance. Apply a couple of coats of shellac before painting: non-glossy, enamel white, flat black, gold, or silver is especially effective. Screw the jaws to a stained plaque (Fig. 168). Add the angler's information in the lower center or lower right side of the trophy.

LETTER-OPENERS FROM BILLS.   A handsome letter-opener—more a curio than a trophy—can be made from the bill of a sailfish or a small marlin. I collect all the bills I can and have fun producing letter-openers that I pass out as gifts to my friends. This type of letter-opener is especially appreciated as an unusual conversation piece.

The process is simple. Cut about 12 inches off the end of the bill. Plan to have 8 inches as the blade of the opener and the remaining 4 inches to

Figure 169. Sailfish and marlin bills make unusual and attractive letter openers. File and sand upper and lower (dorsal and ventral) sides.

Figure 170. Cut the base of the bill away from the solid front position. Polish and add a handle.

accommodate a handle. Use a file to wear down all the roughness of the bill, especially the rasp-like bottom side. Continue to file away, mostly on the top and bottom, until the bill takes on the appearance of a blade with its edges thin and smooth. Now go over the blade with two or three grades of sandpaper—from rough to very fine. When the opener takes on the smoothness of glass, polish it. This can be done with any type of abrasive polish such as rouge and an electrical buffing wheel. I get excellent results, however, by dipping a piece of cheesecloth into alcohol and dabbing it into whiting. Then it's a matter of rubbing it on, applying more alcohol and whiting, and rubbing some more.

File the hind 4 inches of the bill to a shape which will accommodate whatever handle you intend to put on it. My wife Bo found a curious small

Figure 171.   The finished letter opener.

silver umbrella handle in the shape of a duck's head, complete with glass
eyes and ivory bill, at an antique shop that made a most attractive handle
for a marlin-bill letter-opener. I placed some liquid plastic into the metal
end of the handle and pushed the handle end of the bill into it. I held it in
position in a vise until the plastic set.

However, it is not necessary to hunt around in antique shops for an
appropriate handle. If you are handy with a penknife, carve one; or look for
an old hunting-knife handle or a stag-horn handle that can be removed
from a discarded kitchen carving set.

Five or six inches off a tine or prong of a deer's antler can be made into
a beautiful handle. Simply drill a hole in the tine and glue the paper cutter
in it.

CHAPTER TWELVE

Amateur Fish Museums

A mateur nature museums are surprisingly numerous. The urge to collect things is strong within everyone. There are those who collect books, stamps, antiques, neckties, deer antlers, cooking recipes, photographs, bird lists, guns, tools, shrubs, fishing tackle—one can go on indefinitely. Another strong urge is to delve into things of nature; every weekend of the year, throughout the country, hundreds of thousands of people visit museums of natural history. Combine the two—interest in nature and the urge to collect—and a powerful force is born. One of the best ways to satisfy this urge is to build an amateur museum at home.

These home museums vary greatly. My attention has been called to every degree of endeavor in this respect, from a shelf covered with sea shells to entire rooms lined with glass cases holding valuable collections of minerals. All summer camps for children have a nature museum of some sort. Tourist stops in hundreds of places around the country have museums as attractions. Since I am a professional museum man, I tend to examine these various amateur museums with a critical eye. I find that the one great omission in nature museums is fish exhibits—this despite the fact that fishes and fishing draw more popular interest than all the other amateur museum subjects combined! I have scanned all available literature pertaining to fish preservation and exhibition, both technical and popular, and find that fishes are either treated very lightly or ignored completely. No wonder amateur naturalists have omitted fishes in their museums—there has been no encouragement.

The collection and preservation of fishes for amateur museums in nearly every part of the country is easy. The actual collecting of specimens is fun, and the planning and execution of fish exhibits can be interesting and educational. The project is inexpensive. Every summer camp, school, boy-scout organization, and national park museum, regardless of the part of the country where it is situated, should have an exhibition of at least the local fishes.

Figure 172. Fish preserved for displaying in a 10 per cent solution of Formalin (nine parts water, one part Formalin).

As soon as the fish exhibit has been allotted a certain section in the nature museum—a room, cabin, tent, or any other type of shelter—the first thought that comes to mind is mounted fishes, and this is the point at which the fish exhibition idea is usually discarded. Mounted fishes are not necessary, though the camp or school class in crafts can be asked to join the project by making plaster casts of the local fishes. An easy, attractive, and interesting way of displaying fishes is to place them individually in a liquid solution in jars. But let us start from the beginning.

COLLECTING THE FISHES

Rod and Reel.   First, and most important, the collection or exhibition must start with local fishes. Lakes, streams, brooks, ponds, brackish waters, and the seashore all have their share of curious kinds. Of course the most obvious specimens will be fishes that are taken on rod and reel, so there is no problem in securing these. Make an effort to catch at least one specimen of all the known or common fishes. For example, when taking lake fishes include even catfish and eels because, as I will point out later, interesting exhibits can be formed with these also.

Seining.   After all the rod and reel fishes have been collect, attention should be given to the lesser known types that can be taken by other methods. Indiscriminate seining or trapping of fishes, other than for bait, is prohibited by law in most fresh waters of the United States. Nevertheless, all state fish and game departments (environmental protection agencies) are cooperative when an educational project is at hand. A responsible person can obtain such a state permit to collect the fishes necessary for a school, camp, or boy-scout project. Send a letter to the director of your state fish and game or conservation department. In any event, the majority of fishes that would make a good amateur museum collection can be taken legally with rod and reel.

Seining is productive, and collecting in this manner is great fun. Common minnow seines available at most tackle dealers in 6-, 10-, 12-, 15-foot lengths and 4- to 6-foot depths serve well. A ¼-inch square is the usual size of the seine mesh. This type of net has pieces of lead along the bottom and wooden floats on the top. The ends of each side, top and bottom, are equipped with ¼-inch rope extensions which should be tied, at each end, to a broom handle or appropriate lengths of bamboo or tree limbs that are fairly straight. Light-weight electrical conduit pipe can be used also. The collectors manipulate and extend the seine by means of these two handles.

Along the shallows of a lake or seashore, two men can do an efficient job of seining. One works up close to the shoreline while the other extends the seine out directly from shore, as far as it is safe for him to progress. Both collectors then walk along a short distance dragging the lead side of the seine along the bottom. It is important that the seine hugs the bottom as it goes along because fish will try to squirm under it and escape. The seine should be kept at an angle which will ease its progress through the water. However, do not drag the floats under the surface.

Seining must be done at a fairly rapid pace. If progress is slow the trapped fish will hit the seine and then quickly swim along the length of it and escape at the outer ends. After going along for about 10 feet, the person working the deep end of the seine should increase the speed to as fast as he can, without falling into the water. The collector holding the shore end of the seine will have to slacken his pace. In other words, the seine is worked quickly and brought around until the entire line of the seine is paralleled to shore. As the outer man approaches the shore, he must keep the seine taut; there should not be any belly in it. This is the point at which many fish escape. Both men must slide the lead side of the seine, still scraping the bottom, right up to the water's edge. Keep an eye on the float edge of the seine. Do not let it drag under the surface; it should be above and out of the water, or the fish will go right over it as they zoom around frantically when approaching shallow water at the shoreline. The whole action must be continuous.

Often the shore area contains obstructions which make it difficult for two men to scramble out while holding the seine taut with the trapped fish. In this case they should pull the seine out of the water, and both men should fold it in two lengthwise. Then they should walk toward each other folding the seine at arm's length as they go along. In other words, the seine ends up like a bag with the fish in the bottom in the hands of one man.

When working a brook or a stream, the pools with fairly quiet waters are worked the same way as described above. In swift waters, however, a different technique is employed. Three men are required to do a good job. The seine is placed across the stream or brook so that a slight belly or trap is formed. The seine should be held at an angle to offer less resistance to the water. The float side of the seine can be a couple of feet out of the water. Check the position of the lead or bottom side so that it is not over boulders which would leave a space for fish to escape. Now the third man steps into mid-stream, about 10 or 15 feet upstream, and kicks over rocks, pebbles, and stones by dragging his feet along the bottom as he progresses as quickly as possible toward the stationary seine. Two or even three persons can do this for best results. All the small fishes, which were sheltered under and behind the stones on the stream bed, will be carried by the current quickly downstream into the seine before they can regain their equilibrium and again scoot under a rock. When the stone kickers come close, the two men at the seine lift it up quickly with one motion. If the procedure is carried out properly, the collectors will be amazed at the amount of tiny fish life in each haul. Usually, the catch will consist of small minnow-like forms which have never been seen by the average fisherman.

Trapping.   Some types of fishes will not strike a bait readily, or they live in water too deep to seine. For these, a trap can be employed. Occasionally, a regular minnow trap will do the job nicely, the kind that can be purchased at most tackle shops. Simply open the trap, drop in some bait such as fish heads or old pieces of meat, and let it stay in the water overnight.

In salt water I have experimented with different types of traps. I have placed them on the sea bottom around docks and bridge pilings, and I have set them from a rowboat in productive-looking areas in the vicinity of submerged rocks and reefs. I found that the arrow-shaped fish pot used in Bermuda, Puerto Rico, and other islands of the Caribbean was by far more successful than the funnel-shaped trap. Several of these traps can be constructed easily with ¾-inch mesh or chicken wire (Fig. 173). A hauling rope with a red-colored float on the one end is tied to the trap. The rope should be long enough so that it will not be submerged by high water. At one end of the trap, a 6- or 8-inch square opening is cut in the mesh and a wire door attached to it. When the trap is pulled out of the water, it can be so tipped that the fishes fall toward the door and can be removed easily. Also, new bait can be inserted. In salt water, bait which draws fishes is made up of clams and mussels with broken shells, old shells, fish heads, and old meat. Light-colored broken dishes placed in with the bait are an added attraction.

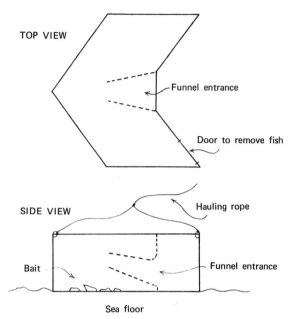

TOP VIEW

Funnel entrance

Door to remove fish

SIDE VIEW   Hauling rope

Bait   Funnel entrance

Sea floor

Figure 173.   Arrowhead shaped fish pot used by fisherman in Bermuda, Puerto Rico, and other Caribbean Islands. It may be constructed entirely of wire mesh.

Fishery scientists supplement seining and trapping methods by other means—electrical shockers that stun the fish, and a poison, rotenone, which kills fishes by affecting their breathing apparatus. However, amateur collectors need not concern themselves with these methods of collecting.

PRESERVING THE FISHES.   Fishes up to the size of a largemouth bass, pickerel, trout, or bluefish can be preserved for display easily in formaldehyde or Formalin (Fig. 172). This chemical can be procured at any drug supply house. Your local druggist can help you. One quart will go a long way. The preserving solution is made with one part Formalin to nine parts water. Be sure to *read* the section on Formalin before working with it (see Chapters 1 and 15).

Professionals use the following method for optimum permanent preservation of fishes. The average specimen—5-10 inches—is kept in the 10 per cent solution of Formalin from two days to a week for adequate fixation. The specimen is removed from the Formalin and soaked in water for two or three days with at least a couple of changes of water. Then the fish is transferred to 70 per cent ethyl alcohol, or to isopropyl alcohol, which is better and cheaper. One change of alcohol is recommended before permanent storage. The reason why professionals remove the specimens from Formalin and place them in alcohol is that over a lengthy period of time the Formalin tends to harden soft parts and soften bony tissue. Also, alcohol specimens are easier to handle for study.

However, amateur museum developers can forget about the alcohol. It is expensive and not absolutely necessary. I have hundreds of specimens which have been kept in a weak Formalin solution for over twenty years, and they are just as good today for display purposes as the day they were first preserved.

The strength of the solution can be varied from the standard 10 per cent. Unusually large fishes (anything bigger than about a 5-pound bass) can be placed in eight parts water to one part Formalin, or very small specimens can be preserved in more dilute Formalin, fifteen to one. Generally, specimens over a few inches in length should have an incision along the abdomen so that the preserving solution can penetrate more easily into the insides (Fig. 174). Make the cut as high up on the side of the abdomen as possible. The right side is usually chosen for the incision. This will leave the left side for the show side with no marks on it. Use a sharp knife; the incision should be at least half the length of the body cavity. Fish over 2½ or 3 pounds should have additional cuts deep into the flesh to facilitate penetration of the Formalin. This can be done from the outside. The specimen will make a neater display, however, if these cuts are made

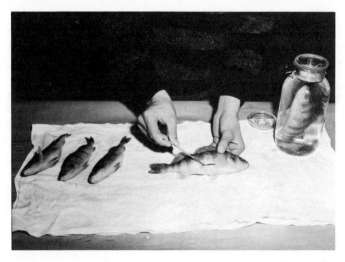

Figure 174. Specimens over a few inches in length, such as these yellow perch, should have an incision along the abdomen so that the preserving solution (10 per cent Formalin) can penetrate more easily into the inside.

Figure 175.   In larger fish, a fairly wide section of skin and meat can be removed to facilitate the entrance of Formalin.

through the slits that were made in the body cavity. Or a fairly wide section can be removed as shown in Fig. 175. Cut long and deeply into the muscle mass on each side of the vertebral column (backbone).

If the specimens are to be stored permanently in Formalin and not alcohol, household borax should be added; it retards shrinkage, hardening of soft parts, and softening of bony material. To 1 quart of preserving solution add 1 level teaspoon of borax. Also, if the specimens are to be displayed permanently in Formalin, it is a good idea (after a couple of weeks) to change the specimen into a new, clean solution of more dilute Formalin (about fifteen to one) to which household borax has been added.

Camp counselors, school teachers, scoutmasters, and others may desire to demonstrate the anatomy of Formalin-preserved fishes to their groups. So that the fishes can be handled, the objectionable fumes of Formalin should be eliminated in the following manner. The local druggist or the high-school chemistry teacher can supply 1260 grams of $NaHSO_3$ (sodium bisulfite) and 840 grams of Na_2SO_3 (sodium sulfite). (There are 454 grams in a pound.) These salts are dissolved in tap water. Then enough water is added to make 5 gallons of solution. The Formalin specimens are rinsed in water before being immersed for a few minutes in this solution. Many specimens can be treated successfully in this bath before a new mixture is required. Do not allow the specimen to dry out in the course of the demonstration. When it has served its purpose, it should be returned to the Formalin for storage.

PRESERVING IN THE FIELD. For the best results specimens should be dunked into the Formalin as soon as possible. Small specimens—up to the size of a 10-inch trout—should be placed in the can or jar of Formalin alive, as soon as they are collected. The fishes do not suffer; they are killed quickly, but they take in the preservative and extend their fins—all of which makes a better display specimen. Care should be used when placing the wiggling fish into the preservative receptacle. When the fish feels the initial sting of the Formalin, it will thrash around, and drops of Formalin may accidentally splash into the collector's eyes. If this happens, bathe the eyes *immediately* in clean water. However, if the cover of the container is held in one hand and clamped down as soon as the fish enters, there should be no difficulty. Obviously, do not attempt to insert a fish into a full jar of Formalin.

Scientists accustomed to working with Formalin may carry glass jars during short collecting trips. In the field, however, the amateur should use a nonbreakable receptacle such as a paint can with a lid or one of the inexpensive plastic-type containers that come in all sorts of sizes and shapes. It is important that any receptacle used in the field be equipped with a lid that cannot be shaken off while traveling. A glass jar of Formalin can be a dangerous thing if broken by accident. When the specimens reach home or the laboratory, they should be rinsed in water to remove any foreign material adhering to them. Then their abdomens should be cut as previously described.

JARS FOR SPECIMEN DISPLAY. Expensive jars are not necessary for display. Food stuffs of all types are packed in screw-top jars. Wide-mouth pickle jars are especially good for fish preservation and exhibition. Restaurants, delicatessens, and school and camp kitchens discard large jars of all types. They are usually happy to cooperate in saving jars for you. Any fish can be displayed to greater advantage if it is placed alone in a jar. Situate the specimen against the glass in the jar so that it can be viewed easily. Fish inserted tail first are easier to remove, head first. Then cover the specimen with the Formalin solution.

A professional touch can be given to each jar by attaching a tag which gives information about the species of fish. Include common and scientific name, locality of capture, date, and name of the collectors. Scientists insert waterproof labels into the jars; waterproof ink is used on the labels. Also, the information on the label is supplemented by other, detailed facts which are entered in a catalog: type of water, vegetation, bottom, shore, distance from shore or stream width, depth of capture, water temperature, air temperature, current, tide, and time of day. Obviously, recording these facts is not necessary for amateur display specimens. However, I strongly recommend that camp counselors, scout leaders, and teachers meticulously employ this procedure with their students, for this presents an unusual opportunity to teach children to observe, and intelligent observation is the basis of every science.

But let's get back to the display jars. Regardless of the different sizes and shapes of the store jars, the collection can be unified by painting all the jar tops one color. A bright color will detract from the specimens; paint them black.

ORGANIZATION OF FISH EXHIBITS.   The display collection may contain many fine specimens, but it will lose most of its value if it is just a bunch of jars on a shelf. Here again, regardless of the persons involved or the type of the collection, scientific principles can be employed. Divide the fish into groups which will denote some type of classification that is easily understood: for example, a group of game fishes, a group of minnows, a group of bottom living fishes. Or they may be divided into stream fishes and lake fishes, or fishes that can be taken by angling with a fly, those that will take spoons or plugs, and those that will take only bait.

Individual lessons in biology can be taught easily by intelligent display of preserved fishes. For example, have two jars side by side, one with a male trout and the other enclosing a female trout. Place the heads in the middle of the jars, against the glass, so that the smooth head and jaws of the female can be compared easily with the angular, irregular jaws of the male. Cut the heads off a largemouth bass and a smallmouth bass and display them in

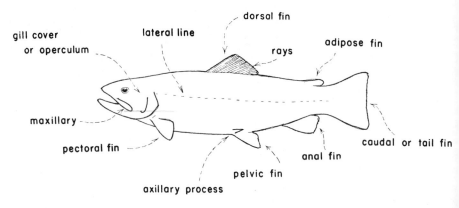

TROUT

Figure 176.   Any person, whether sportsman angler, amateur or professional taxidermist, who works with fishes should be familiar with the nomenclature of the basic external anatomy of the two major types of bony fishes.

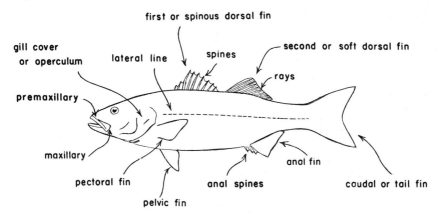

first or spinous dorsal fin

gill cover
or operculum   lateral line   spines   second or soft dorsal fin

premaxillary   rays

maxillary

pectoral fin   anal spines   anal fin

pelvic fin   caudal or tail fin

BASS

Figure 177.   External anatomy of the basslike forms.

individual jars. This exhibit will show that one is distinguished from the other by the length of the maxilla or upper lip which goes beyond the eye in the largemouth. This kind of exhibit is a lesson in observing anatomy more closely.

The fish exhibition in any amateur museum need not end with the collection of preserved local fishes. To the contrary, it should lay the groundwork for further exhibits. The many monthly outdoor magazines contain pictures of all types of fishes that can be cut out and pasted on large cardboards. Individual cardboards can read like this: BIG-GAME FISHES, OPEN OCEAN FISHES, SHORE FISHES, COMMERCIAL FOOD FISHES. Do not clutter up the poster-board exhibits (or any other for that matter) with long typewritten pages of reading matter. It is much better to letter the name under the fish with a colored crayon, then to one side add information that is easy to read from a distance:

THESE FISHES LIVE ONLY IN THE OPEN
OCEAN AND EAT ONLY OTHER FISHES

or

BOTTOM FISHES
EAT WORMS, SMALL CRABS, AND OTHER SMALL SEA ANIMALS

With preserved fishes to supply the professional look and a poster-picture display for treatment of other types of fishes, a fish section or an entire room or tent given to fishes can be more than a fine contribution to an amateur museum; it can be developed, with a guiding hand, into a most important teaching tool.

I have spent over twenty summers at boys' camps as a camper, counselor, staff member, and nature instructor. The zoo and the nature museum are always the most popular projects in camp. During visiting hours on Sunday afternoons, the boys proudly show their parents the zoo and the museum. The exhibits receiving the most attention are the "question" type which can be changed every week. For example, the preserved catfish has a sign under it, "What are a catfish's whiskers used for?" The label under the eel reads, "Did you know that this eel came all the way from the deep waters of the Atlantic Ocean?" Under both captions is added "See the curators for answers." The curators are two or three members of the nature class who walk around, a bit proudly, with a small sign lettered on each peaked cap reading CURATOR.

CHAPTER THIRTEEN

Museums and Expeditions

W hile in the field the curator, preparator, or taxidermist works hard day and night to fulfill the objectives of the expedition or collecting trip. But there are rewards in travel, social life, and opportunities to study. For example, en route to exotic expedition areas throughout the world, I was able to stop and study in many museums and aquariums. During various travels I examined fishes and fish halls in museums in London, England; Paris, France; Brussels, Belgium; Bombay and Calcutta, India; Nairobi, Kenya; Auckland, New Zealand; Buenos Aires, Argentina; Georgetown, Guyana; Lima, Peru; and all the major museums in Canada and the United States, including Hawaii and Alaska. Participation in expeditions has given me exciting experiences, some of them quite dangerous in situations varying from underwater work off Bermuda to the world's highest streams in the shadows of Mt. Everest in Tibet and Nepal.

In this chapter I attempt to convey to the reader an insight into the methodology of field preparation of fishes and an exciting part of the life of a museum taxidermist, whose job it is to collect and preserve fishes and to make molds of them for completion at a future date in the museum laboratory. As I said, field work is tough and the hours are long, but the rewards are great. For the museum scientist, the monetary returns are not overwhelming—in my spare time, I do a bit of commercial taxidermy and much writing for publication to keep the wolf from the door. I would not exchange my expedition experiences, however, for all the money in the world.

THE COLLECTION AND PREPARATION OF FISHES INTENDED FOR EXHIBITION. The purpose of my study of fishes—photographing and preserving them and making plaster molds—was to provide specimens for

Yale University's Peabody Museum and, at that time, the proposed new Hall of Ocean Life associated with the Bingham Oceanographic Laboratory. It was my job to design and execute the fish exhibits. As a focal point in the anticipated great hall, I planned to display a giant manta, or devilfish. The exact replica was to be suspended close to the ceiling with spotlights arranged so that ocean-blue light beams would streak out effectively from within the confines of the silhouette of the enormous aquatic animal. The light fixtures and bulbs would be hidden from the museum visitors' view below. The composition would give the illusion of a manta swimming dramatically close to the surface of the blue sea waters of the open ocean, as they habitually do, thereby creating a spectacular but highly authentic and educational exhibit.

My opportunity to collect a giant manta came when I was assigned as ichthyologist (fish expert) in the Yale-South America Oceanographic Expedition to the currents off the west coast of South America in the Ecuador-Peru-Chile region. These waters were chosen as the site of exploration because they contain one of the world's richest bodies of salt water, including the Peru current, from which to draw materials for each of our three major concerns: biological oceanography, big-game fishes, and museum exhibits.

I was justified in making elaborate preparations to collect a giant manta because I knew we were to see many of them in the oceanographic upwelling along the coast of South America. This region contains a profusion of the small crustacea and other tiny planktonic organisms on which manta feed. The cephalic fins (flexible projections at the manta's head) are an aid in directing the microscopic food into its horizontally elongated mouth. The popular name "devilfish" is derived from these harmless hornlike head fins that give the fish such a monstrous appearance. Mantas are capable of gathering and consuming great amounts of tiny plankton because they have special filtering organs in their mouths which retain the food while the water is expelled through the gill openings.

As every museum fish technologist knows, a fish-skin mount intended for exhibition is highly inferior to one reproduced in synthetic or plastic-like materials cast from a plaster mold. The mold method has another advantage: The mold does not deteriorate and can be stored indefinitely. A polyester resin cast can be produced from it at any future time. Also, more than one reproduction can be made from the same mold—when a school of fish of the same size is intended to be exhibited, for example (see Chapter 3). The skin mount eventually cracks, peels, and becomes sticky as its natural oils ooze out. Invariably, the specimen appears to be stuffed.

Plaster, however, in its original 100-pound packing, is a bulky commodity to handle. And when an expedition is to take place somewhere halfway around the world, it is wise to purchase the material from a source as close as possible to the working site. After exhaustive inquiries into possible South American outlets proved fruitless, I finally obtained the plaster from a supply house not far from our museum. The plaster was stowed aboard the *Marise,* a 25-year-old, 63-foot diesel powered vessel out of Stonington, Connecticut. This commercial fishing boat was converted into a laboratory ship for the purposes of our expedition. The structure of her fish hold had been altered to provide work space and accommodate oceanographic equipment. The plaster from the original packaging was transferred into new 5-gallon cans obtained from a paint distributor. These containers were equipped with wire handles and lids having an underside groove fortified with a gasket. The lip of the lid was made tight by folding down the protruding tabs. The cans were moisture proof and were easily stored aboard the vessel as it was being prepared for its long journey from the Atlantic to the Pacific.

From the list of fishes we were to collect, and taking into consideration the average size of each species, it was a simple matter to calculate the amount of plaster to be shipped. Although the plaster traveled a long journey by sea in the damp hold of the *Marise,* it arrived in Peru in perfect condition. Each day I transported just enough plaster ashore to do the day's work. Tools and materials were kept in a hillside building under lock and key, and were brought to the beach each morning. Such precautions were necessary to prevent pilferage by the natives. As the plaster was used from each can, when the molding took place on the beach at Cabo Blanco, the containers were packed with Formalin-preserved specimens, such as reproductive organs, eyes, fins, and other materials intended for future reference and research.

Fresh water, molding plaster, sisal, and electrical conduit or other pipe (to strengthen the mold) are the basic ingredients of a fish mold. Sterine, a greasy liquid substance that is a mixture of stearic acid and kerosene, is used as a separator between the edges of mold halves. It is prepared in advance and included in the shipment of supplies. A fairly stiff 2-inch brush is used to apply the separator over the edges of the first half of the hardened mold so that the newly mixed plaster for the second half will not bind to it.

All fish possess a protective coating of slime or mucus over their skin that is designed to reduce friction with the surrounding water, thereby enabling them to move smoothly. The mucus must be removed; otherwise plaster next to the skin will not harden completely and details of scalation will be lost. In this case, vinegar was an excellent detergent. A few ounces diluted in a pan of water and applied over the skin with a sponge, rag, or scrub brush will clean most fishes. Oily species, such as bonitos, may require additional treatment. After the water and vinegar mixture is wiped off, a coat of lacquer out of an aerosol can, sprayed lightly over the skin, will effectively seal off the epidermal and emerging subcutaneous mucus and prevent contact with the plaster.

As soon as we arrived at Cabo Blanco I spent the first few days ashore preparing materials and arranging a site on which to work. Salt water does not mix well with plaster and fresh water was not available close to the beach; therefore, we trucked it down from the mountain in 50-gallon drums. The two natives I hired as assistants shoveled level an area of beach that had an abundance of fine, clean sand. Sand, wet through with water, is used to prop up the head and tail of the specimen in a lifelike position, as well as to fill under the fish in order to prevent plaster from flowing below the midline of the body, dorsally and ventrally.

Sisal, a plant fiber that comes baled in long strands, is saturated in plaster and incorporated into the mold to strengthen it after the first or splash coat has completely covered the exposed half of the fish. My assistants were constantly preparing the sisal by pulling it out of the packing and forming loose handfuls to make dipping and complete saturation in the plaster easier.

Our methods of collecting the fish specimens varied depending on the species sought. Small fishes, preserved in bottles containing 10 per cent Formalin, were taken by drag net in deep water, at times in the middle of the night. Other rare species were obtained from the stomachs of big-game fishes that were caught when they came close to the surface after feeding in the depths. Shallow, tide pools, where only a dip net was needed, were also productive. An ordinary minnow seine was employed to capture tiny fishes along the beach. All of the other species intended for museum exhibition had to be taken by rod and reel.

Angling methods depended on the type of fish we were seeking. Big-game and medium-size fishes such as marlin, sailfish, and dolphin were taken by trolling bait on the surface. The bait for big-eye tuna and sharks was drifted at varying depths of about 8-10 fathoms. Grouper, snapper, and other reef-loving species were caught on cut bait brought close to the bottom by lead sinkers. The launch that ferried personnel from boat to boat or from boat to shore and back also served as a fishing vessel for inshore trolling for roosterfish, jacks, cero mackerel, spanish mackerel, bonito, and others. I especially enjoyed hunting for a large roosterfish. There was no mistaking a school of them when they ripped into a concentrated ball of confused baitfish close to the water's surface.

After several weeks of collecting and mold-making, with intermittent hunting for the giant manta, my task was completed—except for the manta. We had observed many of them while we trolled for big game, but I was choosy. I felt that all of the specimens we observed swimming close to the surface were too big. A devilfish we harpooned and lost in the Indian Ocean during a previous expedition had made a lasting impression on me.

It was much smaller than any I saw in South American waters, and therefore I was concerned about trying to harpoon any of the huge awesome forms we saw. Only a few days remained for our field work when, late in the morning, Mr. Anderson, leader of expedition, approached me and said, "Ed, I am afraid that if you don't stick one of these critters soon, time will run out." I replied, "OK, we'll hit the next one."

I had selected Pepito, the most intelligent of the Peruvian fishermen we employed, to be the harpooner. Pete, as I called him, and I had made preparations weeks in advance. He filed the harpoon point to needle sharpness. To the wooden shaft we fastened about 200 feet of ¼-inch manila rope that was tied to a small barrel. The rope was neatly coiled in a box and, along with the harpoon and barrel, secured to the deck ready for action. Previously, with the aid of a penciled sketch, I instructed Pete to strike the harpoon into the wing of the manta. I explained to him that the devilfish then would have full use of only one of the winglike fins, causing it to be unbalanced as it swam and therefore easier to capture.

It was near 3 P.M. when several manta were sighted by Pete, who was positioned at the bow of the *Suzanne V*, one of our fishing craft. I stepped onto the bridge to get a better view. There, dead ahead, were four manta. Captain Bill Fagan eased back the throttle and turned the wheel a bit to port so that we came up on the group of devilfish from the left. I looked them over carefully. They were all close to the surface, just easing along, wing tips now and then protruding above water. To my dismay they were all the same size—huge! It was now or never. I signalled to Pete and returned to the bow, grasping every handhold available en route. He picked up the harpoon. I kneeled on the deck and held the barrel, ready to throw it over the guardrail as soon as the line played out.

The wind pattern during the entire expedition was constant. The early mornings were calm, fishing was comfortable until noon, and then the winds became progressively stronger. At about 4 P.M. they blew to about 20-25 miles an hour and gusting to about 30. As the winds increased in velocity, the waves became correspondingly higher. Pete was having difficulty keeping his balance as he poised the harpoon. The bow was dipping deeply into the trough of the waves and coming up with a sudden lurch. Captain Fagan controlled the boat beautifully to slide us alongside the outermost manta. Pete pulled back his arm, aimed for the left wing, and with a mighty effort cast the harpoon. At precisely that moment, the *Suzanne V* was on the downward pitch of a wave, causing Pete to overthrow the target by about 5 feet. Instead of hitting the wing the harpoon flew directly into the middle of the back of the manta.

To my horror, the manta, instead of shying away immediately from the boat as every fish does, cut across the bow and zoomed off with terrifying speed to the left. I screamed for Pete to hit the deck. He bent down but not quite fast enough. The manila rope tore across his back, taking skin with it. From my kneeling position, and with much help from the adrenalin going through my system, I tossed the barrel across the cabin top with all my strength, like a shot-putter using two arms. Fortunately, the barrel bounced on the port rail and landed in the sea.

At a speed hard to imagine in such an ungainly fish, the manta swam off so fast that the trailing barrel became a mass of white froth that disappeared from view regularly as it was forced through the waves. After the initial burst of speed for about a half mile, the devilfish settled down to a steady fast pace. When I was beginning to think that the manta was going to continue out to sea indefinitely, the barrel paused. The *Suzanne V* came up on it cautiously. For a dozen times or more, the barrel traveled about 100 yards and stopped, another 100 yards and stopped. This was a sign that the devilfish was nearing exhaustion. My strategy was to drain the animal of its resistance without giving it time to sink to the bottom where it would be impossible to pull up.

Now we were all on deck except Captain Fagan, who remained behind the wheel. Pete, who in the excitement didn't seem to mind the ugly skin scrape along his entire back, was standing by with a gaff ready to bring the barrel aboard. Mr. Anderson and his son Jack (who was assistant director of the expedition) were clearing the deck. I went below, brought up my sheath knife, and secured it to my belt from where I could pull it out in a second to cut the rope if necessary. A hundred yards of rope on the deck of a bouncing cockpit attached to more than a ton and a half of unpredictable resistance creates a highly dangerous situation. One simple curl of rope around a wrist or ankle could mean someone being yanked overboard.

Pete reached out with the gaff, picked up the rope and brought the barrel aboard. The rope came in easily, but suddenly, when the manta saw or felt the presence of its enemy, the boat, it took off again. I was close by Pete as he let go of the rope and shied away as it swished over the side. I waited for it all to go before I threw the keg overboard again. The next time Pete started to bring in the line there was no force pulling it away from the boat. The four of us then started to haul in the rope until the enormous black back appeared up close, like some unknown monster of the deep. Although the manta came in without attempting to swim away, it was still very much alive. The harpoon was solidly imbedded in its back, but evidently did not penetrate any vital organ.

It was obvious that towing the manta 40 or 50 miles back to Cabo Blanco by the harpoon line would be impossible. The fish had to be attached to a heavier rope and lashed as close as possible to the transom. Now the seas had built up gigantic waves 8-10 feet high. On our first attempt to pull in the manta, it slid down a wave and came crashing against the gunwale thrashing its enormous batlike wings. About 4 feet of the tip of one of the triangular fins slapped into the cockpit. As the manta started to slide back, Pete tried to impale a big-game gaff into it. The gaff did not penetrate the extremely tough, thick skin; it was jerked from his grasp and lost in the sea. Captain Fagan's groans and curses rose above the noisy excitement.

The manta revived considerably and began to swim again. Jack Anderson and I held a quick conference. A rifle that Captain Fagan had stored below for use against sharks was brought up. Jack pumped about a dozen shots into the head of the manta before it subsided. The sea was red with blood. Everyone's next thoughts were on sharks. Water came into the cockpit every time the manta smashed into the side, heaved by the mountainous waves. I reached out with a rope and tried to tie a couple of half hitches around one of the horns, but that was too dangerous even with someone holding the back of my pants belt.

I finally solved the problem by digging my knife into a thin part of the wing. After several attempts, as the waves pushed the manta in and out of reach, I cut a slit through the wing, forced the rope into it and tied it securely. Then the horns were roped easily. With the ropes fastened to the stern cleats, we began the bumpy, five-hour return trip to shore. Wet and tired, we agreed that our drinks were well earned. It was after 11 P.M. when the *Suzanne V* dropped its anchor at Cabo Blanco, where it stayed overnight with the devilfish tied to it.

Early the next morning, the ropes holding the manta were transferred to the launch. Before the carcass was towed to shore, we turned it by some cumbersome maneuvering belly-side up, because the ventral surface was to be molded, and to turn over the animal on shore would be impossible. The launch dragged the manta towards the beach as far as the shallow water allowed, and then with the help of the men, women, and children of the beachside village, the devilfish was pulled ashore by a single rope. When the bulky body touched sand, it came to an abrupt and most decisive stop. Additional people came to help. We tugged and tugged the ¾-inch rope but we could not budge that massive form. I sat down to rest on the manta, whose body was half under the water. I was beginning to feel uneasy about the situation.

Seeing me deep in thought, the assistant manager of the Cabo Blanco Fishing Club, who was in the crowd of spectators watching from the pier, came down to offer use of his archaic, clanking, rust-ridden panel truck. I looked at his relic and then at the manta. While I was dubiously considering his offer, he jumped up on the donkey-cart road that was two feet higher than the beach. He got into his parked truck and turned it around so its rear end faced the beach. Without waiting for my approval he took the end of the rope, squirmed under the truck, and tied it to the rear axle. With a smile and waving the two-fingered V sign for victory, he hopped back into the driver's seat. He started the engine, and as native behavior demanded, the gas pedal was jammed down to the floor. When the slack in the rope became suddenly taut, the rear axle assembly was ripped from the chassis. The rest of the conveyance came to a sickening, crunching halt in a great cloud of dust about 20 feet ahead of the axle and wheels still attached to the rope.

When the excitement died down, the oil company's pier foreman, who also had been watching the proceedings, offered the use of the company truck. He tied the rope to two cleats bolted to the bed of the vehicle in a way that centralized the pull. He drove slowly. The rope gradually became taut, but when the cleats started to come away from the wooden platform I warned him to stop. He then informed me that it would take only a short time to drive to the mountaintop where the garages were located and return with the company's largest truck geared for heavy duty. After accepting his suggestion, I looked at the manta, sucked into the sand, and it occurred to me that the only way we were going to save that specimen was to break the suction and give the body some momentum in the pulling process.

I walked down the road to where the oil company had a huge pile of odds and ends stored. I selected three 4-inch pipes 8-12 feet long, and several 2-inch by 10-inch planks, 8 feet long. We carted them down to the beach. The pipes were placed ahead of the manta to be used as rollers when we set the planks on top of them. One end of each plank was shoved as far as possible under the carcass. This roller system, with the aid of the huge truck, was a success. The devilfish was dragged up the beach above the high water mark.

It was obvious that a one-piece mold was out of the question. To crate such an extensive mound of plaster and ship it to Yale would be virtually impossible. Therefore, I decided to make the mold in four pieces. Each wing, starting from close to the body outward was to be a separate section. The other two pieces would be the head half of the body including the horns, and the rear half.

First we scrubbed the entire surface of the manta with the water and vinegar mixture, although the rough, sharklike skin was almost devoid of mucus. My next concern with the help of two natives was to make the beast appear lifelike. While Carlos lifted a wing, Enrique shoveled wet sand under it. I prodded and shifted sand here and there until, in my estimation, the great, flexible fins looked as if they were in swimming motion. I did not curve the tips excessively, as mantas often do, because the cast or model was to be silhouetted against the museum ceiling, and if sight of the wing tips was lost, the spectator looking up at it would not perceive the true outline of the fish. The head fins also had to be supported with sand and positioned in a lifelike attitude. Then, more sand was shoveled completely around the manta to form a shelf about 8 or 10 inches wide. The shelf was made smooth by working a wet trowel over it.

After several weeks of experience, Carlos and Enrique acted like pros and were fun to work with. A pile of handful-size clumps of sisal were stacked, ready for use. Two drums of fresh water were at hand, and the ¾-inch pipe used to strengthen the mold was cut to measurement. Carlos sifted plaster into a small washtub, about a third filled with water, until the water could absorb no more. (Plaster would be too lumpy if water was poured into it.) I no longer had to remind Carlos to avoid working his hand in and out of the plaster to smooth it out. Such mixing causes air pockets to form in the plaster, thereby creating holes in the mold.

It is highly important that the first thin splash coat of plaster be applied carefully because it reproduces the skin texture (or scalation in other fishes). Speed in application is imperative. The first coat should not set before the second coat, reinforced with sisal dipped thoroughly in plaster, is applied. As I was flowing the plaster over the horns and head section of the manta, Carlos was sifting plaster into another washtub while Enrique stood by ready to run with the first tub down to the surf to wipe it clean of plaster before it hardened. The second batch of plaster was mixed more heavily than the splash coat. Its consistency was almost as thick as whipped cream and remained where placed. The entire section was built to a thickness of about 1½ inches, leaving about 4 inches of the edges free of sisal.

While the plaster was still soft the sides were marked with the aid of a length of mason's twine. Then, a spatula was quickly employed to remove the excess plaster from the straight line along each side. As soon as the plaster hardened, a liberal coating of sterine was applied to the edges facing the rear, against which the back or tail part would be molded. After the wing portions were molded in a similar manner, the four sections were individually reinforced with pipe. We bent the pipe to fit the contours of each piece and tacked it down at intervals to the hardened plaster with sisal dipped in freshly mixed plaster. Other pieces of pipe were bent to meet the shape of the entire mold, that is, the four sections. These lengths of pipe were marked to correspond with points on the mold: they would be used as guides or templates when assembling the four parts of mold in the museum laboratory in preparation for casting.

We worked for 14 hours under a cloudless sky. Darkness was approaching. The mold was finished and safe to leave overnight. I was exhausted. The task of cleaning the tools and the area was given to Carlos and Enrique while I took off my khaki trousers and canvas shoes saturated with plaster and sand, and changed into fresh ones. One of the natives rowed me in a small dugout canoe to the *Vagrant* where a hot shower and a cold drink were never more appreciated.

The next morning, as the sand was shoveled from under them, the wings of the manta dropped partially away from the mold. With the help of several onlookers, the mold sections were lifted off the carcass, carried to a waiting truck, and transported to the top of the mountain where they were stored in a shed. Plaster molds, before the water has had time to evaporate out of them, are extremely heavy, but in the tin-roofed, ovenlike shed they dried out rapidly. The other fish molds previously brought to the shed were loaded for the return journey aboard the *Marise* and were secured in the hold formerly occupied by the plaster and other materials.

After caring for the molds, we returned to the beach to measure and weigh the carcass. From wing tip to wing tip the span was 18 feet, 6 inches. Like all sharks, skates and rays, the manta has a cartilaginous skeleton (no true bone); therefore, it was not difficult to hack through the true skin, the cartilage, and blubberlike meat to separate the wings from the body. Each of the three pieces was roped and dragged into the water at high tide. The launch towed them to the end of the pier where the pier manager, expertly maneuvering a huge crane, hoisted them out of the water onto the pier. Each piece was weighed. (The crane and scale were the same equipment used in 1953 to lift and weigh Alfred Glassell's world-record 1560-pound black marlin, which still remains the largest game fish ever taken on rod and reel.) The three pieces totaled 3360 pounds. Considering dehydration and loss of fluids in dismembering the body, it is safe to assume that the fish originally weighed about 3500 pounds.

The expedition's fleet and personnel departed but I stayed on for a few more days to supervise the crating of the manta molds. I lodged at the Cabo Blanco Fishing Club overlooking a magnificent stretch of beach and ocean where the birds awed me with their profusion and variety. Each evening before a late dinner I enjoyed a couple of hours surfcasting, not for specimens but for fish that I took pleasure in giving to the natives.

I hired a local carpenter, showed him the molds, and explained how they should be braced inside the crates. He grasped the situation and told me that it would be no problem because he was experienced in crating machinery and other heavy materials for shipment to the United States by the oil company. But the next day I was shocked when he arrived with a truck load of rough-cut mahogany, beautiful planks 2 feet wide, 12 feet long, and an inch thick. When I found my voice, I told him that it would be a sacrilege to use such material to build crates and that there was no way that I could pay for such fine wood. He said, "But senor, this is the cheapest wood that comes to the mountain." And so it was, much less expensive than the poorest grade of wood used for making boxes and crates in New Haven.

Several months later, the crated molds arrived by ship and were unloaded at a pier in Brooklyn, New York. After the customs details were facilitated by a broker I arranged for a truck and driver from Yale's transportation department, and we traveled to Brooklyn to claim the shipment. We returned with the gigantic crates to the receiving platform of the Bingham Oceanographic Laboratory. It took me several days working carefully to remove the nails from the mahogany. I salvaged each of the planks and used them to wainscot the dining room in the house I was building at the time. There remained enough of the attractively grained wood for me to construct some furniture and a 12-foot-long bar in our basement barroom named, in the terminology of the Atlantic salmon fisherman, "The Home Pool."

Sequel: The assistant manager's panel truck was not a total loss after losing its rear axle and wheels. The engine was salvaged and sold to a local saw mill. The axles and wheels became the mobile part of a donkey cart. The expedition chipped in $50.00, more as a tip for his services than payment for the demise of the vehicle. Also, I presented him with all the tools, wire, pipe, and other surplus materials from our beach operations. He was totally happy.

Epilogue: If the circumstances were such that the devilfish could not have been dragged high enough on the beach to mold it, would all the time and effort to the project have gone to waste? The answer is "no."

The project was assured of success when the manta was towed to shore. If we found it impossible to pull the carcass above the limits of the high water mark, I would have turned to the alternate plan of securing reference material in order to sculpt, in the museum laboratory, a close reproduction of the manta. A clay model would simulate the original animal, and the plaster mold could be constructed.

HISTORY OF MUSEUM PREPARATION.

The preservation of animals so that they can be displayed indefinitely is not a recent idea. A review of the history of museum exhibition portrays the gradual evolution of methods and results over the past several hundred years, from a crude beginning of "stuffed" specimens to the present magnificent works of art in great halls of famous museums.

It is interesting to investigate the origin of early attempts at animal preservation. There are, of course, many examples of the caveman's crude use of animal skins; he formed them over mud and rocks to imitate live animals for ritual purposes. For the same reason the Egyptians, who pioneered the art of embalming, preserved animals in their entirety. One may search further and note that in Peru there is recorded the use of preserved bird skins for ornamental purposes as early as A.D. 1200. The Spanish conqueror of Mexico, Cortez, informs us that Montezuma, whom he dethroned, possessed robes covered with the skins of trogons and other birds of brilliant plumage. Unfortunately, history records these facts only because they are associated with the outstanding figures of the times. However, it may be safely assumed that there must have been stuffed birds

Figure 178. The manta, captured by harpoon, weighed more than 3300 pounds and measured 18½ feet from wing tip to wing tip.

Figure 179. After the fight off Cabo Blanco, which lasted for four hours, the giant manta is towed ashore.

Figure 180. The people of Cabo Blanco helped drag the huge specimen ashore.

Figure 181. Planks and rollers were placed under the manta. A rope was tied to a truck and everyone pulled.

Figure 182. We dragged the manta above the high water mark. The local school was let out so that the children could see the manta.

Figure 183. The author securing the reinforcing rods with sisal dipped in plaster.

Figure 184. The finished mold as it appears after two days of hard labor in the broiling sun.

Figure 185. The sand is being shoveled from under the wings so that they can be pulled from the mold. At the same time the electrical conduit pipe is cut at the seams of the four piece mold.

Figure 186. One wing section has been removed.

Figure 187. The head mold, which includes cephalic or head fins, is being removed.

Figure 188. The pectoral fin of this striped marlin is cut off and molded separately.

Figure 189. A shelf of sand has been built up to the midline around the entire fish, except its bill (the original bill is used in the polyester resin mount). Gaff marks have been repaired and the body is brushed off.

Figure 190. The first or splash coat is applied.

Figure 191. The entire mold is given another layer of plaster reinforced with sisal and then the reinforcing pipes are attached.

Figure 192. The sand is removed from the tail end of the mold so that the tail fin can be grasped and pulled away from the mold first.

Figure 193. To get away from a stiff boardlike mount, the striped marlin being molded on the shore of Otehei Bay, New Zealand, was first positioned in a body curvature that depicts action.

Figure 194. The completed mold after the marlin was removed from it.

Figure 195. The molds are stored under cover until dry in order to lighten them. Then, local carpenters were employed to crate the specimens in preparation for shipping them to the museum at Yale University.

in existence during a period when work with bird skins was so popular. Five centuries before Christ, Hanno, a Carthaginian navigator, collected gorilla skins that were preserved for generations. Actually, as far as it can be ascertained, this is the earliest recorded attempt to preserve an animal skin for a purpose other than ritual. One of the earliest recorded examples of an entire mammal mounted for museum exhibition occurred in Italy. A rhinoceros was "stuffed" for the museum of Ulysses Aldrovandus in Bologna in the sixteenth century. Later it was transferred to the Royal Museum of Vertebrates in Florence.

This is not the place for an extended thesis on the evolution of museum preparation and exhibition, but I have pursued the subject fully and followed the recorded word of improvements by date and step by step. This research on museum development can be accomplished with satisfaction on bird and mammal mounting. But what about fish?

In contrast to developments in bird and mammal taxidermy, tracing the history of fish mounting is a frustrating and fruitless task. Why is the recorded word on the progress of the subject so rare? Simply because the preservation and mounting of a fish skin was always discouraging, never satisfactory. There was no progress to record.

The date of an early attempt at fish mounting comes from an unexpected source. Shakespeare's *Romeo and Juliet,* first performed in 1596, gives us a clue:

> I do remember an apothecary,—
> And hereabouts he dwells, which late I noted
> In tatter'd weeds, with overwhelming brows,
> Culling of simples; meagre were his looks;
> Sharp misery had worn him to the bones:
> And in his needy shop a tortoise hung,
> An alligator stuff'd and other skins
> Of ill-shaped fishes.

The extract not only gives a date for the early presence of fish taxidermy but also accentuates the fact that centuries have passed and still many of our best museums continue to display "ill-shaped fishes."

I have been fortunate in being able to visit the best museums of natural history around the world. To my knowledge there is not one which has a hall of fishes that compares in standard to the great halls of birds, mammals, or vertebrate paleontology in many museums today.

There are several reasons why this is so. The preparation of fishes for museum exhibition was difficult. Mammals can be modeled to perfection; their skins are preserved indefinitely by tanning, and coloration is no problem since it is naturally retained. The feathers of mounted birds cover skin damage and built-up anatomical blunders; at least most of the museum birds of today look respectable. Most of the museum fish specimens are mounted skins, which are almost invariably monstrosities. A mounted fish skin eventually splits and oozes grease; the fins crack; and the head shrinks to distortion, and attempts to rebuild it with wax are unsatisfactory. Some museums use models. Most of these models are rigid and have no character; their fins are flat and without expression, cut from Celluloid or other material. And nearly all of the fishes are painted by persons who have never seen the specimens alive.

CRITERIA FOR MUSEUM FISH MOUNTS.   Today there is no excuse for poor fish mounting and poor fish exhibition. True colors of fishes are easily recorded with today's variety of wonderful color films. The greatest boon to the art of fish displays was the advent of plastics and other synthetic materials. Any fish can be molded in plaster and cast accurately in durable artificial materials. Tranportation of working materials to the field of operations and return of plaster molds is no longer an obstacle.

But, let's start from the beginning. I would like to speak to the museum curators, preparators, and commercial taxidermists like a Dutch uncle. Before delving into the mechanics of producing accurate, durable, lifelike reproductions of fishes in synthetics, it is important to know what a live fish really looks like. This is not a ridiculous statement, for I'm surprised to see that when detail of fish anatomy is involved, even some trained scientists fail to observe intelligently. I would like to suggest a few pointers for scientists and technicians to keep in mind when pleasing, accurate reproductions are desired.

Body.   The most common fault found in fish mounts, and one that preparators and commercial taxidermists insist on perpetuating, is the contorted body. These gentlemen think that to twist a fish's body dorsoventrally—from topside to bottomside—depicts action. No such thing. The fish is no longer a delight to look at; it has its back broken and its curvatures are crippled. The fish appears to be in agony. Whenever I see such a mount, I have a feeling that I should hit it over the head with a club to stop its misery.

Watch a fish in the water; its body movements are from side to side, not from top to bottom. Look at an action photograph of a hooked fish (one that has not been faked); again, the body is bent laterally. Next time you see a movie of a marlin or any other fish jumping, note that its head and tail swing from side to side, not up and down. In other words, it is physically impossible for a game fish to bend into violent curves which bring its head and tail down or up at extreme angles. The anatomy of the fish will not

Figure 196. The natural curvatures of a fish's body are lateral, that is, from side to side as shown above—not twisted up and down into grotesque forms seen in so many mounted fish.

permit it. A *slight* downward or upward bend in the tail region is fine, and any mount will have plenty of action by turning its head or tail, or both, slightly away from the wall (Fig. 196).

Fins.   Next to the body itself, the fins are the most noticeable pieces of anatomy on a fish. With the proper angulation and curvature placed in the fins, any type of action desired in a mount can be accentuated. But for heavens sake, *do not stretch the fins* to their extreme width and *do not force them away from the body.*

It is practically impossible to find a mount that does not have its fins dried flat, stretched to their fullest and away from the body. The fish appears to be frozen in fright—like a funny cartoon which shows a man's hair standing straight up when he sees a ghost. Again, think. When a fish is stationary or swimming, its fins are undulating in movement; there are smooth curves within the fins which do not stretch violently. The fins do not open and close like a Japanese fan. Form pleasing curves in the fins, whether you dry them in position or reproduce them in plastic. For example, you can portray a fish swimming swiftly by positioning the fins backward, especially the dorsal fins. Fishes use their tails and body for propelling themselves through the water. The fins are mostly stabilizers in one respect or another.

Mouth. Here again, the tendency is to exaggerate. The open mouth is forced wide beyond all reasonable action. This fault is especially apparent in the largemouth bass. Have you ever seen a mount of this species which did not have its mouth pulled wide into distortion? If you have, it's a rarity. Why do taxidermists stretch a fish's mouth into ugliness? Wouldn't it be more pleasing to open a mouth partially? Every mounted largemouth bass I have seen looked worse than if it were trying to regurgitate a big bullfrog and failing in the attempt. We know it is a largemouth bass because the end of the maxilla (upper lip) reaches backward beyond the eye, not because its mouth has been stretched to appear like the opening of a sewer pipe.

Eye. The eye of a mounted fish is nearly always too large, and it is easy to find out why. Next time you see a fresh fish, observe its eye closely. Notice that the eye is in a ball that fits into a socket. Also note that the extreme width all around the eye is not as wide in diameter as the eye socket. A taxidermist removes the eyeball and replaces it with a glass eye that fits exactly into the entire socket and which, of course, is much bigger than the original eye. To do a good job on the eye of a mounted fish, a portion of the eyeball should be indicated and the width of the eye proper measured. A glass eye of the same size should be inserted.

Color. It is more difficult to criticize the paint job of a mounted fish. First, all species of fishes go through different shades of intensities of coloration at one time or another. Often two specimens of the same type of fish, inhabiting waters only a few miles apart, will be different in coloration. If an angler is accustomed to fishing in one area, he may consider a mount of the same species of fish, taken from another area, as being inaccurately painted. Second, a mounted fish is not easy to paint. Anyone expecting to do a professional job must have natural ability plus accurate knowledge of the coloration of the live fish.

One of the most important steps in painting mounted fishes is to secure color transparencies of the fish while it is alive or as soon as it is dragged out of the water. The photos must be supplemented by color notes. Unless the artist has confidence in his knowledge of the subject, the mount will be inferior. Read the suggestions for techniques of recording color of the specimen in the field in Chapter 1 and techniques of painting in Chapter 6.

MUSEUM FIELD WORK. Museums of the world have had a more or less standard procedure in caring for fishes which were to be used for display. Fishes taken in distant areas were skinned, packed in salt, and sent to the museum. If the specimens were not too large and taken closer to home, they were packed in ice and shipped. Some museums working directly in the field made molds of a few large fish such as sharks.

However, the only method that will produce superior mounts is to make plaster molds of all fishes as soon as they can be brought ashore. Second best is to freeze the fish as soon as possible (see Chapter 1). Every museum mount should be cast in a durable synthetic. Even skins of fishes that are difficult to obtain should never be mounted. Instead, the skin should be filled and modeled as accurately as possible to its former shape. A mold is made of it and then cast in one of the new plasticlike materials. Incidentally, this is also an excellent way to save old mounts of skin specimens. Model the shrunken head and lips with modeling clay; then proceed with the molding as if the fish were a fresh specimen.

Foreign Shipping, Materials, and Customs.   The entire procedure of molding fish in the field is not as difficult as it may appear. I have made molds of fishes, varying in size from a ½-pound snapper to a manta ray weighing 3300 pounds, on distant beaches around the world in Africa, Alaska, New Zealand, and South America. Every mold arrived in excellent condition at Yale University. Since my methods have evolved over the years—mostly by trial and tribulation—I am sure that curators, preparators, and others doing this type of field work will find the following information of unusual value.

If the expedition is to take place outside the shores of the United States, be sure to secure all of the supplies here. Ship them by freighter to their destination. I purchased plaster of Paris of a foreign make in another country and regretted it. The plaster was inferior, and I had a bad time trying to produce first-class molds. Only No. 1 molding plaster should be used. I have experienced this type of exasperation several times; therefore, regardless of what fine reports I may receive concerning availability of supplies in remote areas, I ignore them and ship plaster, sisal, pipe, Formalin, tools, wire—everything. Sometimes the heavy material such as plaster can be purchased and shipped from a point closer to embarkation, but this procedure also presents complications.

Through correspondence, or better yet through an agent, make contact with customs officials at the point of arrival in the foreign country and with the customs people in the United States, where the returning materials will come. To demonstrate the necessity of checking well in advance with customs in this country, I relate the following experience. During an expedition to Africa, I shipped out 3300 pounds of plaster. But, when the plaster returned to this country, in the form of fish molds, the trouble began. Some of the customs people insisted that Yale University pay a duty on the molds (which would have been considerable with a return of over thirty molds of all sizes). The customs officials could not understand that the plaster was the same material which left the country— only in a different form. After weeks of correspondence and trips to New

York, everything was finally untangled. Much time can be saved and wear-and-tear on the nervous system avoided if you make previous contact. However, be sure to get everything in writing; keep a file on all these transactions. Ship the materials months in advance. It is a rare freighter that departs and arrives on time, and be sure there is a capable agent at the other end to store supplies and equipment until an expedition member can take over.

Do not arrive "cold turkey," so to speak, and expect to put in a good day's work on the beach. If possible, plan to come a week or so early to prepare the work area. It is even more important to use that time to advantage in gradual acclimation to the sun. I have worked all day, many times, on beaches near the equator where there was not a cloud in the sky, and temperatures hovered at the 100-degree mark. Yet I felt no ill effects, simply because I had exposed myself to the sun gradually for longer periods of time, over a week or so, before working on the beach.

Plaster of Paris should be packed according to distances involved, length of time in the field, and facilities for transportation. For example, if the expedition will be in the field for several months and many fishes are to be collected, I advise shipment of the plaster in 30-gallon drums that will weigh 220 pounds each when filled with plaster. Specify "export type," provided with rubber gaskets and convenient lock-type covers. I shipped fifteen of these drums to Africa.

Wherever possible, however, it is more advantageous to ship the plaster in 5-gallon pails, available at most paint-distributing concerns. These pails are provided with metal handles and wooden grips which make the plaster easy to handle in the field. The lids are equipped with metal extensions that close the pail snugly when bent down, and rubber gaskets are included.

The pails are excellent as receptacles for returning Formalin specimens. After the specimens have been preserved thoroughly in Formalin, they can be packed in wet cheesecloth without being sent in Formalin. The pails will be in no danger of leaking Formalin, they will be much lighter in weight for shipping, and the specimens will not be harmed. For additional protection and moisture, I prefer to place wet sisal (other material can be used) around the specimens so that they will not damage one another during transit.

Each pail filled with plaster weighs close to 40 pounds. I usually pack four to a crate for shipment. During one expedition to South America, we had one boat sailing from Connecticut; therefore, I simply trucked the pails uncrated to the dock and loaded them on—fifty pails.

Amount of Plaster per Fish.   For a collecting expedition to Alaska, I shipped sixteen pails of plaster packed in four crates. This was enough to mold three big salmon (35-40 inches, up to 52 pounds), two medium salmon (20-30 inches), two rainbows (30 inches each), two sheefish or inconnu (24 inches each), one grayling, one northern pike, one dolly varden or Arctic char, and one mackinaw or lake trout. A 45-inch or a 45-pound fish will require approximately one 5-gallon pail of plaster per side, or two pails for the fish.

As a further example of amounts of plaster per type of fish, the following specimens are some that I collected in the Bahamas: 7½-pound barracuda—40 pounds plaster or one pail; 16-pound Nassau grouper—60 pounds plaster or one and a half pails; 5-pound blackfin tuna—40 pounds plaster or one pail; 36-pound amberjack—80 pounds of plaster or two pails.

I have enumerated the above as a rough guide. If one knows the type and number of fishes to be collected, the amount of plaster to be used can be ascertained fairly well. Always take a few extra cans. No. 1 Red Circle molding plaster comes in 100-pound bags. I have the bags sent to the museum laboratory where the plaster is transferred to the 5-gallon pails and crated. Three 5-gallon pails will accommodate a 100-pound bag of plaster with room to spare.

Water Supply.   Fresh water is necessary to mix the plaster. When molding freshwater fishes, there is no problem. However, salt water expeditions require a makeshift laboratory on the beach with a supply of fresh water handy (another reason for early arrival on the scene). This is the way I do it. Two empty barrels or oil drums are secured and placed near the spot where the fish are to be molded. Pick a spot which harbors clean sand, with no excess pebbles and shells. I always correspond with a contact man in advance concerning this type of problem, because a receptacle of this sort may be difficult to produce at short notice in a primitive area. Then I hire two or three natives and form a bucket brigade to fill the drums with fresh water. Or I may make arrangements to have the water trucked to the beach. Use this water to mix plaster, but have your native helpers run to salt water, which should be only a short distance away, and clean the plaster out of the pans in the surf. A scrub brush or a handful of sisal will facilitate removal of the plaster that is beginning to set. With a bit of joshing and an approving word now and then, I find that natives develop easily and quickly into valuable assistants.

Mold Reinforcement.   In the field I always reinforce the mold. After the first or splash coat covers the fish, I apply another layer of plaster which has been strengthened with sisal. The sisal is torn or pulled away from the bale in convenient handfuls, dipped in the plaster so that it is thoroughly saturated, and carefully placed along the mold until the entire fish and the built-up shelf around it are covered. Sisal or tow is a strong hemp or fiber obtained from plants. I always have the sisal ready, that is, torn from the bale in small chunks, before mixing the plaster.

A two-piece mold is made of fishes up to about the size of a 75-pound specimen, or up to the point where fish and mold can be turned over to work the other side. However, fishes such as bluefin tuna, marlin, or sailfish have to be produced with a one-side or one-piece mold. Usually, it is possible to apply the plaster beyond the midline of the belly and head because the body of the soft fish can be removed, with some manipulation, from the mold. In the laboratory, a mold that continues beyond the midline of the back and belly can be chipped away to facilitate removal of the cast from it. When such a cast is exhibited, it will appear as a whole fish.

The mold is further reinforced with pipe. Conduit pipe is ideal for the purpose. This pipe is strong but light in weight and can be cut easily with an ordinary hacksaw. Also, it can be bent without trouble to fit roughly into the outside contours of the mold. The pipe is attached to the mold by spots of sisal dipped plaster, in three or four places along each piece. Both sides of the mold area treated in this manner.

When the mold has set and the fish removed, the halves are placed together and tied with a piece of strong wire at each end. A mold of this type is surprisingly strong, but do not give it unnecessary abuse.

Crating Molds.   A local carpenter should be employed to start crating the molds before the expedition has terminated because the procedure requires time and supervision. If two or three small molds are packed in one crate, they should be supported with wooden crossbars and wedges so that no damage occurs from contact among them during shipment.

Allow the molds to dry out as much as possible in the open air or in a shelter that has its windows or doors open during the day. In Guyana, where it rained almost every night during our stay, I had my native assistants on a schedule, carrying the molds into the protection of a shanty toward nightfall. They returned them outdoors, to the sunshine, in the morning. Molds lose a great deal of weight when the moisture leaves them; dry molds are not only easier to handle but the shipping bill will be much less. Air freight, of course, is charged by weight. Cargo vessels, according to their shipping formulas, usually charge by whatever is greater—the size of the crate or its weight.

Setting the Fish for Molding.   When preparing the fish for molding, natural turns and twists can be easily incorporated into the body by shoveling sand into strategic places under the fish. Producing a good mold is a mechancial affair; anyone who has the ability to work with his hands and who does not mind working hard under uncomfortable conditions can learn to construct them in the field. However, manipulating the fish into

Figure 197. Spectacular but accurate curvature can be obtained in the mount. The mako shark above was molded in this position on beach sand after it was caught.

190

correct position for molding is another thing and requires some knowledge of fishes plus an artistic eye. Of course, in the case of a specific fish for a specific exhibit, the fish would have to be molded according to preset plans by the curator. If the curator is not in the field, the preparator should be armed with sketches and notes as to the position the various mounts are to take. The great advantage of producing museum mounts from molds is that lifelike and true-to-form specimens can be produced.

Fins. Do not waste precious time in the field with tasks which can be accomplished in the museum. For example, I do not mold the pectoral and ventral fins on the spot; instead, I cut them from the body with scissors or hacksaw. (Do not cut so close as to remove a piece of body skin; otherwise, fluids will ooze out and prevent the plaster from setting in the area around it.) Then, I spread and tack the fins on pieces of wood and place them in a pan of 10 per cent Formalin so that they float, fins down. After the fins have been preserved in position, in a day or two, I remove them from the wood, wrap them in cheesecloth, add a tag, and then insert them in a bucket of Formalin until time for shipment. Incidentally, I usually preserve heads and other fins also. They are often invaluable for reference points in finishing the cast. Shark jaws, barracuda heads, or any other head with prominent dentition should be removed from the original head and preserved, so later they can be inserted into the head of the mount.

BIG-GAME FISHES. For best results the mold should be made as soon as possible after the fish is caught. However, big-game fishing boats are usually too far out to sea to return immediately with a specimen. Also, nothing would be gained if the anglers returned at midday rather than toward evening. A full, uninterrupted day is required to construct a mold of a larger fish such as a marlin.

When the fish is removed from the boat, it should be placed on the dock, cleaned with buckets of water, and then wrapped with a double layer of potato sacks saturated with water. If the weather is unusually warm, the abdomen can be injected with a 10 per cent solution of Formalin to prevent undue spoilage overnight. Buckets of water should be thrown over the wrapped fish again before retiring. Of course, if a large ice plant is handy, that is where the fish should be stored overnight.

Never leave the specimen in the water tied to the dock. Not only will the action of the sea damage the fish against the pilings, but decomposition will set in faster. Also, sea life that is active at night may chew on the specimen. If the fish is not covered with wet sacks overnight, it will shrink and shrivel and be practically worthless for a good mold in the morning. Arise as soon as the sun breaks the horizon and try to get the plaster on the fish in the cool of the morning.

Figure 198. The cast of the same shark in the museum laboratory.

If the curator or preparator is not a fisherman, he should nonetheless be aboard the fishing craft every possible moment that it is working out at sea. To be aboard to observe fish in action is one of the most important parts of the job. Ideas for exhibition displays will be gained, and color photography of the live specimens, plus notes, will be possible. Last but not least, the specimens can be cared for aboard the craft, and it is necessary regardless of the size of the fish. Small fishes should be wrapped in wet sacks and placed in the bait box. Large fishes that lie in the cockpit also have to be covered with wet burlap and occasionally wetted down with buckets of salt water. A specimen exposed to sun and wind can be ruined in a short time.

One point to keep in mind—you may instruct the captain or mate to look after the specimen, and in all good faith he will agree to do so. However, as every angler knows, the captain and mate have their hands full, looking for fish, rigging baits, handling the boat, and gaffing the fish. Therefore, the specimen will not receive any attention once it is on the deck of the boat, regardless of how important it is to the museum. Furthermore, it is unfair to ask a boat crew to look after specimens. In any event the preparator or curator, who has an opportunity to discuss fish with experienced anglers, will be that much more valuable to the institution that employs him.

Obviously, I have omitted the step-by-step methods of the entire procedure of molding and casting because it is treated in detail in Chapters 2, 3, and 4.

CHAPTER FOURTEEN

Repairing Fish Mounts

Although it is usually only the broken fins that require attention on a mounted fish, it is possible to do a major repair job on any part of the trophy. Skin mounts always need repair after being up on the wall, even though they may not be damaged from force. When the skin shrinks it cracks; grease will ooze at the base of the fins and tail. If the fins are artificial but the body skin original, a space will develop where they join. A cast of a fish, regardless of the kind of medium, will demand the least attention over the years. As a matter of fact, a cast requires repairing only when physical damage occurs.

FINS.   Fins with pieces broken off should be removed entirely and replaced with a new set. If the trophy is a skin mount, obtain fins from another fish, position them between two pieces of paper board, and keep together with paper clips until dry. The bases to accommodate the fins on the mount will have to be cut or drilled out. Wrap a thin layer of cotton, more if necessary, around the base of the fin and dip it into a good glue. The drilled hole in the mount may also require cotton dipped in glue. Brace the fin in position until the glue has set. If the mount has a wooden body, a few brads will hold the fin; but remove the brads when the glue has set. The cracks where the fin meets the body may be filled in with melted beeswax. The wax can be smoothed with a hot tool or an electrical pencil available from art shops. Apply a thin coat of shellac to the repaired area before painting.

If the fins or the tail are cracked between the rays and otherwise not damaged severely, they can be brought back to look normal by reinforcing them with cheesecloth and tissue paper. On the backside of the tail or fin, glue a piece of cheesecloth of the right shape. On the show side, glue a single sheet of tissue paper cut to the appropriate size. The fins and tail make a better appearance if their hind edges (where the rays branch out) are irregular. Therefore, arrange the ragged edges (tear, if necessary) of the cheesecloth and the paper so that they will meet with the irregular edges of the fins. Use a glue with some glycerin in it for flexibility (formula 7). When the glue has set, cut the excess cloth and paper away from the sides of the fin. A pair of scissors will do it. Shellac the repaired fins before painting. Torn or split fins can be repaired also by painting them, when thoroughly dry, with liquid Celluloid, on both sides. Place a piece of tissue paper on the backside and paint over it with more Celluloid. White shellac may be substituted if liquid Celluloid is unobtainable. Incidentally, this procedure may be used to reinforce the tail and fins of a freshly mounted fish after the fins have dried.

Any damaged fins on a plastic mount should also be replaced with new ones. Cut the fin off close to the body with a bandsaw or a hacksaw. Use a drill to cut through the body of the mount for the fin base. Cast the fins and anchor them as described in Chapter 4. Fins cast in polyester resin can be used to replace damaged fins on any type of fish mount.

HEAD. The head of a skin mount will shrink. If it was not brought out to its original contours with wax (by the original taxidermist), it should be done. If the head has been waxed upon the original mounting and is cracked, do not attempt to patch it. Instead, dig and scrape away all of the old wax and remodel with fresh wax. Place a piece of beeswax in a double boiler. When it melts apply the wax to the head with a brush. When enough wax has been placed on the head, work it into shape by scraping a knife over the high spots. With a sharp tool carve in the necessary lines around the gills and lips. Rub down the head with cheesecloth dipped in turpentine to smooth the head. Apply a thin coat of shellac over the waxed head before painting.

BODY. Often the scales on a skin mount will lift. In order to remedy the situation, it is necessary to remove the paint. Apply a standard type of paint remover until the paint is soft, and then wipe it off with a rag. Place some wet cloths over the scales until they soften and return to their normal position. Wipe the excess moisture off the fish and then brush on a thin coat of glue. When the glue has dried thoroughly, coat the entire fish with shellac (thinned 50-50 with alcohol) before painting (see Chapter 6). If the mount does not have too heavy a layer of paint, it will not be necessary to use paint remover. Scales will soften quickly if moisture is applied to the underside of the upturned scales.

If the body skin is cracked, it should be glued back to the mannequin with a good contact cement. If there is a slight separation where the crack occurred, it can be filled in with melted beeswax. Scrape away the excess wax when it cools and then brush on the shellac before painting.

The inside of the mouth, if open, usually requires additional attention. Dig away all old wax; apply fresh beeswax (brushed on hot and melted);

model into the desired shape with scraping tools and a hot iron; smooth with a cloth and turpentine; apply shellac before painting.

It is usually better to give the mount an entirely new paint job rather than attempt to patch up areas. Paint fades, and it is difficult to match an old paint job with fresh paint.

CHAPTER FIFTEEN
Materials and Formulas

I n the old days, taxidermy and museum preparation incorporated all kinds of formulas and mixtures, and most of them were secrets well guarded by the individuals using them. Today a fresher attitude is taken, at least in museums of natural history, and information pertaining to any part of museum preparation is gladly given. Also, there is less need for formulas and mixtures concocted in the laboratory. Today there is an amazing array of easily obtainable, inexpensive, and durable materials which are a great boon to anyone interested in taxidermy, museum preparation, amateur museums, or fish mounting.

Furthermore, there is no need for long, impressive lists of "official tools" required for doing the work; this is especially true in producing fish mounts and other fish trophies. Discarded pots and pans, old kitchen spoons and dull knives, sharp penknives, scissors, and frying pan spatulas are the type of "fancy tools" required. The other tools which may be necessary are the common saw, file, hammer, and pliers.

The different materials needed for constructing fish mounts can be purchased at local stores which deal in hardware, drugs, chemicals, paints, laboratory supplies, and mason supplies. Glass eyes, tow or sisal, and other specific materials can be obtained from one of the taxidermy supply houses listed in Chapter 16.

PLASTER OF PARIS. Plaster of Paris should be "Grade A" or "Number 1" molding plaster. It is available in packages weighing up to 100 pounds. This white, powdery material is procurable at most mason supply houses, lumber companies, art shops, and paint stores.

SISAL. Also called tow, hemp, sisal grass, or sisal hemp, sisal is a strong fiber obtained from the leaves of certain plants. All taxidermy supply houses have it in stock. It is available in small quantities as well as by the bale. Sisal is also known as "machine compressed manila casting fiber." A compressed bale will supply enough sisal to strengthen hundreds of plaster molds.

WOVEN GLASS AND FIBERGLASS.   Woven glass, filter cloth, fiberglass, or glass fiber cloth is available in various weights and sizes of strand and mesh, and usually may be purchased at a store that carries polyester resin. It is sold by the yard. Fiberglass matting (composed of short fibers pressed to a flexible back) may also be used.

CONDUIT PIPE.   I have found that an excellent reinforcement for plaster molds, especially in the field, is thin-wall conduit pipe (⅝-inch inside diameter). It is obtainable at electrical supply houses and comes in 10-foot lengths.

For shipping to distant areas, I cut it into 5-foot lengths and bind the pieces together into packages that can be handled easily. Then I wrap the individual bunches of pipe with burlap sacks and insert each end of the package into a sack so that the individual pieces of pipe will not slip out.

PLASTICS AND RESINS.   There is a wide variety of synthetic or plasticlike materials on the market today that can be used for casting, and anyone interested may find it worthwhile to experiment. A search into the advertising section of telephone directories will produce names and addresses of companies dealing in plastics and resins. Write to them for information concerning self-setting plastics.

Nearly all boat supply dealers carry polyester resins. These resins, combined with fiberglass, are used extensively for repairing and reinforcing boat hulls. The same resins—usually packaged in pint, quart, and gallon containers—are excellent for producing casts of fishes. The resin, when mixed with a small amount of "hardener" or "activator" in a separate container, will set hard in about 20 minutes. A gallon will go a long way. Directions for proper mixing are printed on the container labels. There are different brands on the market, and any dealer in boat supplies will gladly give you all the necessary information about the resin he carries.

Another product which can be used for experimenting in casting fishes comes in paste form and can be troweled directly into the mold; it is usually referred to as plastic paste.

FORMALIN.   Formalin is a colorless liquid with a pungent odor and vapors that are intensely irritating to mucous membranes. It is a preservative and a disinfectant. Formalin is a saturated aqueous solution of formaldehyde gas in water, about 37 per cent formaldehyde by weight.

A 10 per cent solution is usually for preserving fishes: nine parts water to one part Formalin. An 8 per cent solution may be used for large fishes, and a less potent solution of 15 per cent may be used for small specimens.

Formalin may be purchased in most chemical supply shops and is inexpensive. It usually is contained in a fairly rugged bottle. Great care should be taken, however, so that the bottle does not break during transit. A full-strength solution of Formalin spilled on the floor of a car will force its occupants to leave. The only way to alleviate the situation is to douse the area repeatedly with water, and then with formula 3. Then the area may be doused again with water.

Formalin should always be treated with respect. If splashed into the eyes by accident, permanent impairment of vision may occur unless the eyes are bathed with fresh water quickly and repeatedly.

Rubber or plastic gloves should be worn if Formalin specimens are to be handled for any length of time. If a specimen is to be changed from one container to another, a rinse of the hands in water will suffice, but gloves are definitely recommended.

Glue a label marked **POISON** prominently on the receptacle and, of course, keep it under lock and key where children cannot touch it. If jars with fishes preserved in Formalin are displayed, children should not handle them without supervision. It is imperative that the jars be so placed that no one can knock them off the shelf accidentally.

When transporting Formalin, I pack the jars in a strong wooden box with a hinged top and provision for a padlock. If the Formalin is shipped, I screw the top down as an added precaution. The box is divided into wooden compartments, each wide enough to hold a jar of Formalin with excelsior packing around it—including the bottom. Before the top is closed, pack more excelsior in a layer covering the tops of all the jars. Include enough packing so that when the cover of the box comes down, there is absolutely no indication of jar movement within. I have sent Formalin in this way to such distant places as India and then back again with jars full of specimens, without breaking.

Formalin is a wonderful preservative. Its use certainly should not be curtailed because it is a poison. This chemical is perfectly safe if common sense and caution are exercised while handling it.

STERINE.   Sterine is a greasy, liquid substance that is excellent as a separator in preventing freshly mixed plaster from adhering to plaster that has set, as in a two-piece mold. It is also used on table tops when working with plaster. Plaster is easily scraped from an area that has been covered with sterine. The solution is prepared by mixing stearic acid and kerosene. Simply place some powdered stearic acid in a jar and add kerosene until it is well mixed into a smooth consistency. The sterine should not be so thick as to be lumpy. It is best applied with a brush. Keep it in a closed jar when stored. Sterine thickens in a cool room; warm it near a radiator and the consistency will thin.

Stearic acid is a product derived from the fat of beef cattle. It is obtainable in powdered form or block form. If available only in the latter condition, it has to be scraped into a receptacle of kerosene by using a bent hacksaw blade. Chemical supply houses carry stearic acid. A pound is sufficient to make a mixture that will serve many molds.

ALUM.   Alum is an astringent material. It is mixed with water and used (in this instance) to facilitate the setting of plaster of Paris over the fluids and slime that may remain on a fish's body after cleaning the specimen in preparation for molding. It is available at any drug store. A handful in a small pan of water is enough to treat both sides of a medium-size fish.

GLYCERIN.   Glycerin, also known as glycerol, is a sweet, oily, nearly colorless liquid obtainable at drug stores or chemical supply houses. It is viscous and often added to glue and other materials to make them less brittle.

ASBESTOS.   Asbestos, dextrine, and whiting are the main ingredients in mixing a batch of casting compound.

Asbestos, also called earthflax or mountain cork, is a white or gray mineral and has wide use in fire- and acid-resisting materials. Plumbers and furnacemen use it to insulate pipes. For fish preparation, ground gray asbestos is best. It is an inexpensive material also known as asbestos cement. I picked up a one-pound package of "asbestos cement" at a local paint shop; a note on the package read "avoid creating dust, breathing asbestos dust may cause serious bodily harm." Asbestos is also available in 50-pound bags.

Papier-mâché, available at all taxidermy supply shops, may be used instead of asbestos.

DEXTRIN.   Dextrin is a carbohydrate found in nature in the sap of plants. It has adhesive qualities and is soluble in water; it is often used as a substitute for gum arabic. It also comes in large bags and is inexpensive.

WHITING.   Whiting is a finely powdered washed chalk used as a pigment and for polishing. It also makes a fine filler in many substances; it is inexpensive and available at paint shops.

CAB-O-SIL.   Cab-o-sil is the commercial name for fumed silica. It is commonly referred to as ground glass and is available in different textures.

This ingredient is an exceptionally fine filler for polyester resin and is procurable from Cabot Corporation in Boston, Massachusetts.

CELLUCLAY.   Some taxidermists use celluclay, which is a prepared type of papier-mâché. This preparation is a popular item in art classes and is available in art supply stores. The Celluclay Co. Inc., located in Marshall, Texas, produces this item.

SILICONE RUBBER.   This fluid substance when mixed with a catalyst or hardener and a filler, is used to make rubber molds including fish. If it is not available in your area try Dow Corning Corp., Midland, Michigan 48640.

MOLD TEX FILLER.   Used primarily as a filler for rubber molds, it may also be used as a filler for plaster and epoxy resin. This substance is produced by Tandycrafts Inc., Fort Worth, Texas 76107.

OTHER SUPPLIES.   All of the following are available from Adhesive Products Corp., 1660 Boone Avenue, Bronx, New York 10460:
   Adrub RTV (for making flexible molds)
   Kwikmold Latex (for making rubber molds)
   Manzini Liquid Casting Compound
   Alpex Casting Resin
   Pulverized Latex Filler
   Polyester Resin

FORMULAS

1.   Polyester Resin
     Whiting as a filler (amount depends on consistency desired)

2.   Polyester Resin
     Whiting and asbestos (about half as much asbestos as whiting)

3.   Formalin Odor Dispenser
     1260 grams sodium bisulfite
     840 grams sodium sulfite
     5 gallons tap water
     Dunk Formalin specimens in this solution for a few minutes.
     (There are 454 grams in a pound).

4. Wax for Brushing into Molds
    "Parawax" or paraffin—5 ounces
    Rosin (colophony)—8 ounces
    Carnauba wax—1 ounce

5. Wax for Pouring into Molds
    "Parawax" or paraffin—8 ounces
    Carnauba wax—2 ounces
    Rosin—2 ounces
    Turpentine or benzine—1½ drams

6. Separator in Casting
    Vaseline—one part
    Beeswax or petroleum wax—two parts

    Shave wax into a jar of kerosene; let stay overnight; add the Vaseline.
    Should be consistency of cold cream. Strain through cheesecloth if
    necessary. When the shellac in the mold has dried, apply the
    separator with your fingers. Rub it into every detail. The separator
    will spread smoothly with the warmth of your hand. Be sure to work
    it in well, and do not apply an excessive amount—wipe away until a
    thin but effective coat covers every bit of area.

7. Glue—Glycerin Solution
    Glue—9 parts
    Glycerin—1 part

    Warm glue in double boiler; when thin, add glycerin and mix
    thoroughly. Always warm glue for thinning and stir before applying.

8. Casting Compound
    Dextrin—5 pounds
    Whiting—5 pounds
    Asbestos—5 pounds
    Water—1 gallon
    Glycerin—3 ounces
    Carbolic acid—1 teaspoon

    Mix whiting and asbestos in a large receptacle which has room to
    spare. Boil the water and add dextrin gradually. Keep stirring or the
    dextrin will settle to the bottom in chunks. Add glycerin and car-
    bolic acid to dextrin and water. Pour the solution into the basin or
    bucket which holds the asbestos and whiting. Mix thoroughly.

This mixture can be stored in an airtight container for an indefinite period of time. I usually prepare a batch that will fill a 10-gallon crock, and then I remove the compound by the panful whenever necessary.

When ready for casting, add water and mix well until the mixture is well thinned out. Then add plaster of Paris and knead the compound until it reaches a heavy consistency that can be spread easily with a spatula.

CHAPTER SIXTEEN

Taxidermy Supply Shops

Archie Philips
(Fiberglass reproductions for sale)
200 52nd Street
Fairfield, AL 35064

Bob Davis
(Fiberglass reproductions for sale)
2717 N. Tamiami Trail
North Fort Myers, FL 33903

Bob's Taxidermy Supply
321 N. Perry Street, Dept. M
Johnstown, NY 12095

Bradson Supply
1908 Bugle Lane
Clearwater, FL 33516

Chicago Latex Products
1030 Morse Avenue
Schaumburg, IL 60172

Clearfield Taxidermy
Dept. MT-8
603-605 Hannah Street
Clearfield, PA 16830

Dan Chase
Taxidermy Supply Co., Inc.
Route 2, Box 317-A
Baker 7, LA 70714

J.W. Elwood Supply Co., Inc.
1202 Howard Street
Omaha 7, NE 68102

Fiberglass Coatings Inc.
P.O. Box 10636
St. Petersburg, FL 33733

J.M. Hofmann Co.
963 Broadway
Brooklyn, NY 11221

Jonas Bros. Inc.
1037 Broadway
Denver, CO 80203

Kulis Freeze-Dry Systems
725-M Broadway
Bedford 7, OH 44146

Mackrell Taxidermy Inc.
Concordville, PA 19331

Modern Taxidermist Magazine
1-21 Bruchac Drive
Greenfield Center, NY 12833

Northstar Freeze-Dry Systems, Inc.
P.O. Box 439-D Industrial Park
Pequot Lakes, MN 56472

Penn Taxidermy Supply Co.
Dept. M-15
Hazelton, PA 18201

Professional Taxidermy Training
721 Park Street
Ogdensburg, NY 13669

Reel Trophy Inc.
(Books on airbrush, acrylics,
and oil painting instruction)
P.O. Box 19085
Portland, OR 97219

Smallwoods Taxidermy Supplies
28 Waugh Drive
Houston 7, TX 77007

Southerland's Taxidermy Supply
Route 2, Box 160
Wilmington, IL 60481

Taxidermy Supply Co.
Route 1
Bassier City, LA 71112

Tohikan Glass Eyes
Box 121
Ottsville 7, PA 18942

Terry Walton
Taxidermy Supplies
Route 4, Box 715
Salisbury 7, NC 28144

Van Dyke's
Woonsocket 7, SD 57385

Index

212
Index

excelsior body, 82
full mold, 92, 93
half mold, 84, 85, 87
one side, 82
reinforced, 89
removed from mold, 90
repair of, 194-196
wood mannequin, 82-84
Skinning, 7, 8, 74-80
Slime removal, 10
Soap separator, 41
Spears, 73, 141-144
as letter openers, 147-149
marlin, 141-144
mold of, 73
preparation of, 143, 144
preserving, 141
sailfish, 141-143
sawfish, 143
swordfish, 141
as trophies, 141
Specimens:
collecting, 151-154
display in formalin, 157
field care of, 5, 157, 158
formalin, 199
freezing, 2, 4
frozen, 4
preparing for formalin, 199
preparing for molding, 10-12, 18
preserved, 5, 6, 154
protecting, 2, 5
removing from mold, 175
salting skin of, 8
show side of, 4, 10, 18, 86
shrinkage of, 7
spoilage of, 2
storage of, in formalin, 6, 7, 154-157
Spoilage, preventing of, 2
Steric acid, definition of, 199, 200
Sterine:
definition of, 199, 200
preparing, 199
separator, 199, 200
Supplier, 204

Tails:
preserved, 140, 141
as trophies, 140, 141
Taxidermy supply shops, 204, 205

Trap, collecting by, 153, 154
Trophies:
bills, 141-143
heads, 138-140
letter openers, 147-149
photographs, 126-137
shark jaws, 145-147
silhouettes, 110, 111
spears, 141
special, 138
tails, 140, 141

Vaseline:
separator, 19
formula, 202
Vinegar, 10

Wax:
bending, 45
brushing into mold, 202
carnauba, 202
cast, 41-45
cementing, 44
colophony, 42
color, 44
defects, 44
fillers, 42
finishing, 44, 45
fins, 45
formulas, 42, 202
painting, 44
pouring into mold, 44
reinforcement, 43
removal from mold, 43
repairs, 44
resin, 42
seams, 44
separator, 41
trimming, 44
whiting, 42
Whiting:
definition, 200
in wax, 42
Wire hangers:
plaster cast, 40
wax cast, 43
Wiring mold, 23, 26
Woven glass:
material, 198
plastic cast reinforcing, 56, 59, 61